Geography 21 Copymasters

Simon Ross

Published by HarperCollins*Publishers* Limited
77–85 Fulham Palace Road
Hammersmith
London
W6 8JB

www.**Collins**Education.com
On-line support for schools and colleges

First published 2001

© HarperCollins*Publishers* Limited 2001

ISBN 0 00 711445 1

Simon Ross asserts the moral right to be identified as the author of this work.

British Cataloguing in Publication Data

A catalogue record for this publication is available from the British Library

Copymasters designed by Janet McCallum

Cover designed by Derek Lee

Project managed and edited by Susannah Baccardax and Ron Hawkins

Illustrations by Jerry Fowler

Production by Kathryn Botterill

Printed and bound by Martin's The Printers Ltd, Berwick upon Tweed

www.**fire**and**water**.co.uk
The book lover's website

CD-ROM
You will find a CD-ROM inside the back cover of this book. It contains all the material from the book, plus four extra worksheets. By using cut-and-paste methods, you will be able to adapt the material for your own use, if you wish.

Licence: When you buy this pack you are buying a site licence. You may make as many copies of the CD as you need for use in your institution. Of course, you may not pass copies on to teachers in other institutions, or sell on any of our material under any circumstances.

Reading the CD: You need Acrobat 4 to access the files on this CD.

Printing from the CD: You will achieve a better quality print, particularly for maps, if you deselect the 'use printer halftone screens' option in the print dialog box.

The *Geography* 21 *Copymasters* are intended to complement the three textbooks in the *Geography* 21 series. They have been written to fulfil a variety of needs and it is hoped that their standard format and clear design facilitates easy and effective photocopying and classroom use.

Using the *Geography 21 Copymasters*

The *Geography* 21 *Copymasters* can be used either at their current size (A4) or they can be enlarged/reduced. Indeed, the mapping exercises often benefit from enlarging to A3 to give pupils more room to work. This is particularly true for activities such as plotting hurricane tracks. You may prefer to 'cut and paste' the resources to suit your own requirements.

Space has been allowed for answers to be written on the sheets themselves, though you may prefer your pupils to write their answers in their own books. This applies particularly where activities are being used to stretch the more able and where more space needs to be available for free response than exists on the sheets. An alternative approach is to use the activity sheets as 'rough' copies, which the pupils subsequently use to make their neat write-ups.

Several of the *Copymasters* lend themselves to extension work, either as homework exercises or to help stretch the more able. Some are linked specifically to the textbooks – for example, mapwork exercises – while others are discrete and form additional case studies.

Features of the *Geography 21 Copymasters*

There are several key features of the *Copymasters*:

- Activities designed for testing understanding, knowledge and skills – for example, using OS maps and Atlas maps, and drawing cross-sections. The completion of such exercises can form a record of a pupil's progress and achievement.

- Base maps for activities in the textbooks – for example, plotting rural land uses on Cherry Tree Farm (Book 2).

- Blank country outlines for plotting geographical features and for use in mapping statistical information.

- Tables of key statistics both for countries of the European Union and for selected countries from around the world. Such data can be used to support the study of individual countries or to compare countries. The data can also be used in mapping exercises – choropleth mapping, for example.

- Several activities involve the use of ICT. Many activities encourage pupils to use the Internet to research topics, such as refugees, earthquakes and tornadoes. Pupils are also encouraged to use ICT in recording their findings, by using Word documents and the various 'draw' facilities, for example. You may wish to discuss the cross-curricular opportunities presented by using such materials. It may be possible for an ICT department, for instance, to use the *Copymasters* as part of its ICT programme.

- The use of statistics is encouraged, and several activities are devoted to plotting statistics in the form of graphs and diagrams (bar charts, pie graphs and line graphs). Simple statistical tests are also introduced, such as Spearman's Rank.

The *Geography* 21 *Copymasters* should prove to be a valuable resource and provide useful support for the *Geography* 21 series.

Contents

Contents continued

The World

Atlas Map A activities

1 What is the name of the land below sea level in East Anglia?

_____

2 Find the South Downs in south-east England. What is the famous headland formed where this range of hills reaches the coast?

_____

3 What is the height of Kinder Scout in the Pennines?

_____

4 Dartmoor in south-west England lies between which two rivers?

River 1: _____

River 2: _____

5 What island is separated from mainland Scotland by the Firth of Clyde?

_____

6 Where is St George's Channel to be found?

_____

7 Which is further north, the Firth of Forth or the Firth of Lorn?

_____

8 Which is further east, Flamborough Head or Spurn Head?

_____

9 By how many metres is Ben Nevis higher than Ben Macdhui?

10 Which river flows into the River Severn?

_____

11 What is the name of the river that flows towards the west from the Cambrian Mountains?

_____

12 What range of hills lies between the Rivers Tweed and Tyne?

_____

13 What is the name of the main island that forms part of the Shetland Islands?

_____

14 To which group of islands does South Uist belong?

_____

15 Choose any area, place or river labelled on Atlas Map A that you have enjoyed visiting and write a few sentences saying why you like it.

Area: _____

Reasons for liking it: _____

_____

_____

_____

_____

_____

_____

Atlas Map B activities

1 Three of the following cities have nearby airports. Can you find out which they are?

CITY   TICK/CROSS

Southampton   _____

Norwich   _____

Swansea   _____

Manchester   _____

Inverness   _____

Leeds   _____

Aberdeen   _____

2 What is the name of the town that is situated on the English/Scottish border?

_____

3 A friend has sent you a postcard from Wales, but has incorrectly spelt the name of the holiday resort town as 'Abberistwith'. How should it be spelt?

_____

4 Use the scale to work out the straight-line distance between Liverpool and Manchester.

_____

5 What is the name of the main town on the Isle of Man?

_____

6 If you travel by train from Bristol to Exeter, which town do you pass through?

_____

7 The following towns are all on the south coast of England. Try to complete the spaces in their names.

_ _ i _ ht _ n

_ l _ m _ u _ h

_ a _ _ b o _ _ n _

_ _ v _ _

P _ _ _ e

8 Which of the following three cities in northern England is furthest west? Tick the answer.

York   _____

Sunderland   _____

Bradford   _____

9 What is the name of the town that is situated on the English/Welsh border?

_____

10 Choose one of the towns or cities on the map and describe what you like or dislike about it.

Name of town/city:

_____

Reasons for liking or disliking the town/city:

_____

_____

_____

_____

_____

UK outline map

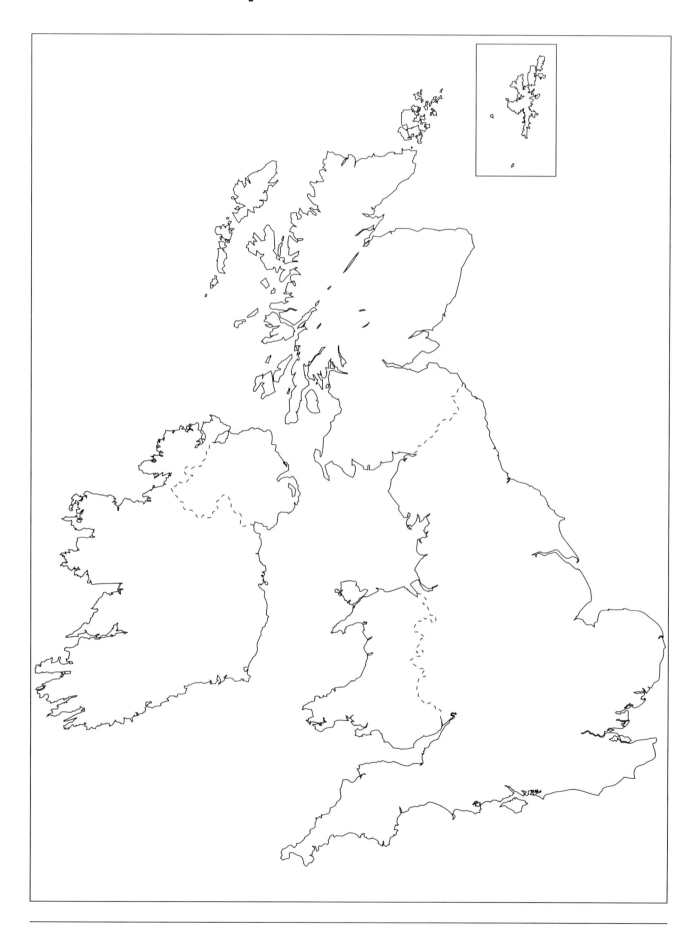

Major cities, rivers and uplands in the UK

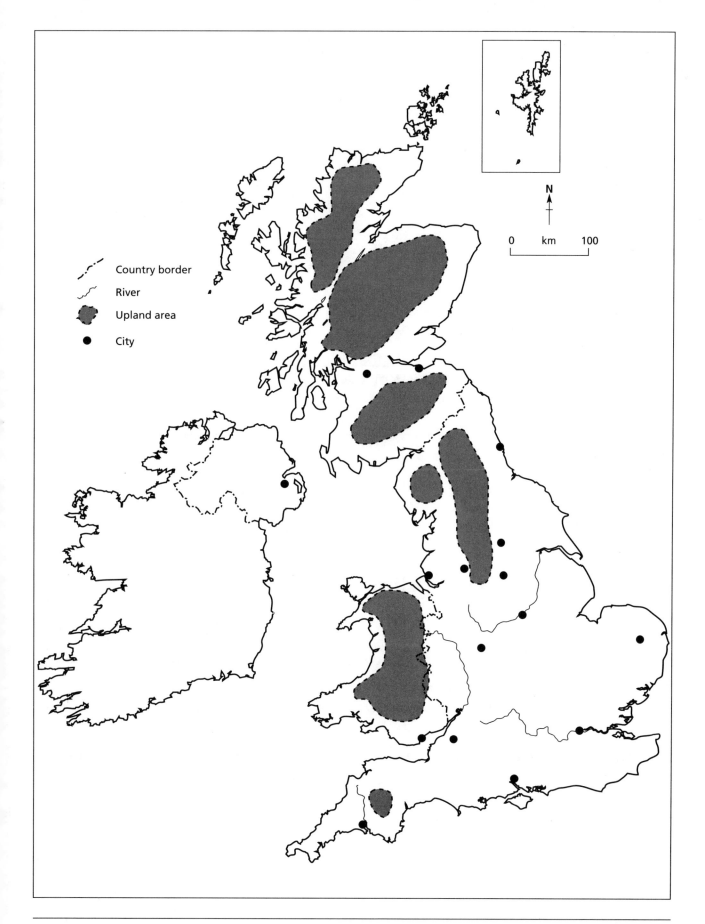

Drawing a cross-section

In Skills Box 6 (page 25) you learned how to construct a cross-section. Here is a chance for you to have a go at drawing another one!

1 Draw a cross-section from X to Y on Figure 1. Use the graph axes in Figure 2 to plot your height values, and then join the points with a freehand curve.

2 Locate and name the following features, using symbols if you wish:

- River Prune
- Tickle Wood
- Bat Wood
- Moose Hill
- flat valley floor
- steep slope
- gentle slope

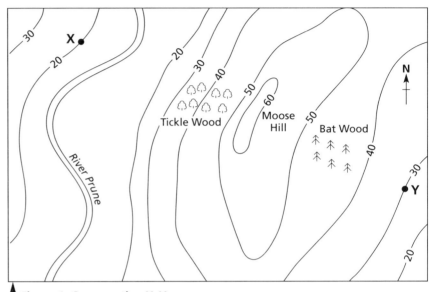

Figure 1 Cross-section X–Y

Figure 2 Height values for cross-section X–Y

3 Which wood is found on the steepest slope?

_____

4 In which compass direction is the steepest slope facing?

_____

OS mapwork revision test

The following questions refer to Figure 2.3 on page 15.

1 What is found in grid square 5178?

_____ (1)

2 In which grid square is West Fen Farm situated?

_____ (1)

3 Give the six-figure grid reference for the following:

a church with a tower in
Little Downham   _____ (1)

b Half Acre Farm   _____ (1)

c the level crossing just
north of Chettisham   _____ (1)

d the roundabout at the
junction of the A10(T)
and the B1411/B1382   _____ (1)

e the windmill to the east
of Little Downham   _____ (1)

4 What is found at the following grid references?

a 523790 _____ (1)

b 558833 _____ (1)

c 550813 _____ (1)

d 547834 _____ (1)

e 549819 _____ (1)

5 Locate the A10(T) in 5381. Does it pass through a cutting or is it raised on an embankment?

_____ (1)

6 A boy has to travel from the village of Stuntney (5578) to go to school in Little Downham. The following paragraph describes the route he takes. Use the map to follow the route and complete the gaps. All grid references (GR) are six-figure references.

From Stuntney we join the main road

(A_____) and drive in a _____

direction towards Ely. We join the Ely

by-pass at a roundabout at GR_____.

At the third roundabout the A_____ joins

from the south. Just beyond the next
roundabout we pass a motel at

GR_____. At GR 528809 we cross

_____ Way. At the next

roundabout we take the first exit

and join the B_____ travelling in a

_____ direction towards Little

Downham. After entering the village we

pass a church with a _____

on the right-hand side of the road. My
school is just after the church at

GR_____.   (10)

7 Calculate the distance travelled by the boy from his home in Stuntney to his school in Little Downham.

_____ (2)

Total marks: 25

Choosing a settlement site

The ground on which a settlement is built is called its 'site'. There are many factors that affect people's decisions about where to build a new settlement. These reflect the need for defence, shelter from the weather, fertile land for farming, woodland to provide building materials and food, and water for drinking.

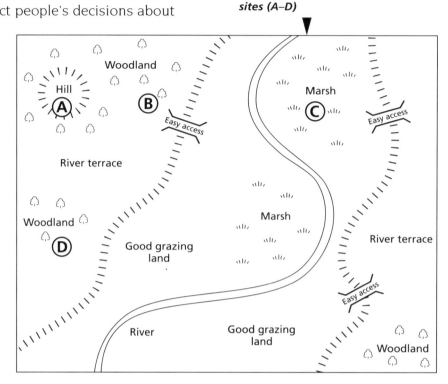

Figure 1 Four possible settlement sites (A–D)

1 Imagine that you are the leader of a group of people wishing to build a new settlement. You have discovered an area of land (Figure 1) and now have to decide where to build your new settlement. After many hours of heated discussion (and a good deal of wailing and gnashing of teeth) four possible sites (A–D) have been identified by your group.

Complete the table on the right (Figure 2), giving the advantages and disadvantages of each of the proposed sites A–D.

Figure 2 Advantages and disadvantages of settlement sites A–D ▶

Site	Advantages	Disadvantages
A		
B		
C		
D		

2 Which of the four sites A–D do you think is best and why?

Site: _____

Reasons for choice:

_____

_____

_____

3 Do you think there is an even better site? If so, show its position on Figure 1 and say why you think it is so good.

_____

_____

_____

_____

Mapping the weather

The weather recorded in different parts of the UK can be mapped using familiar symbols (Figure 1). Such maps help us to see at a glance how the weather varies across the UK.

1 Use the symbols in Figure 1 to map the weather recorded for 12 June (Figure 1.4, page 45) on to Figure 2. Alternatively, you may wish to use information from a recent newspaper. You will need to refer to Atlas Map B on page 10 to help you to locate the places.

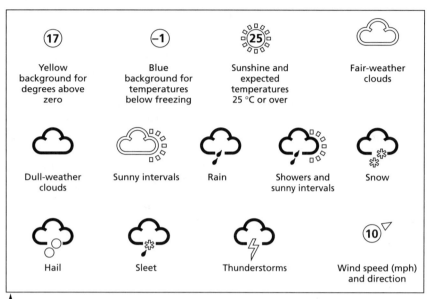

▲ *Figure 1 TV weather symbols*

2 Write a few sentences to describe the weather across the UK as shown by your map.

_____

_____

_____

_____

_____

_____

_____

_____

_____

_____

_____

Figure 2   UK outline map ▼

Research into thunderstorms on the Internet

Having learned about the formation of thunderstorms on page 47, this activity involves you in finding out more about the hazards associated with thunderstorms.

The aim of your research is to produce a poster or booklet describing the following two aspects:

1   The hazards associated with thunderstorms, including heavy rain, lightning strikes, and hail damage. You should be able to find some amazing pictures of hailstones.

2   Actions that can be taken by people to reduce the effects of thunderstorm hazards.

Record information in a notebook or use the 'cut-and-paste' option on your computer. Do not resort to simply cutting and pasting printed sheets! Your teacher will tell you how many photographs you are allowed to print and use.

Here are some Websites to get you started, but add any that you find for yourself when conducting an Internet search.

Websites

www.nssl.noaa.gov/reasearchitems/thunderstorms (National Severe Storms Lab.)

www.nssl.noaa.gov/edu/ltg (good for lightning)

www.ncdc.noaa.gov (National Climatic Data Center)

www.spc.noaa.gov (Storm Prediction Center)

www.fema.gov/library/thunderf.htm (Federal Emergency Management Agency)

australiansevereweather.simplenet.com (fantastic photos)

(N.B. The above sites were correct when going to print but unfortunately they do change, so be prepared for some of them failing to connect).

National Climatic Data Center
"World's Largest Archive of Weather Data"

About NCDC | What's New / Hot | Search | Help

In the Spotlight

2001 Satellite Conference

Satellites In Our Everyday World

Find Weather Station/Data (city/station name)
[   ] Search

Locate NCDC Products by
Most Popular Products | User Description
Weather Station/City | Category / Type
NVDS (Keywords, Maps, Regions, etc.)

Online Store
Products | Subscriptions | Order Status

Browse by Data Type
Satellite | Climate | Radar

Discover Information About Climate
Research | Monitoring | Extremes & Events

Climate graphs

Use the data in Figure 3.3 (page 51) to draw climate graphs for Onich, Cromer and Plymouth using the axes in Figure 1 below. On each graph, colour the precipitation bars blue and use red to indicate the temperature line.

1 Look at Figure 1.

a At which location is the highest annual rainfall recorded?

_____

b Suggest reasons why there is so much rainfall at this location.

_____

_____

_____

2 Look at Figure 1.

a Which place would you visit if you wanted to enjoy a relatively mild winter?

_____

b Suggest one reason why the winters here are so mild.

_____

_____

_____

3 How does the temperature pattern for Cromer compare with that of Plymouth?

_____

_____

_____

◄ *Figure 1* ▼

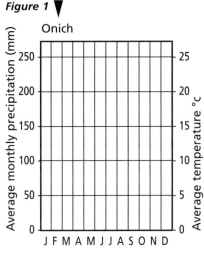

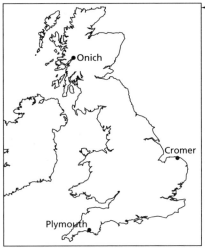

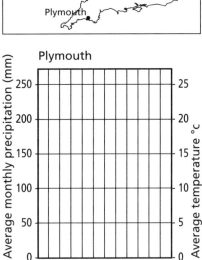

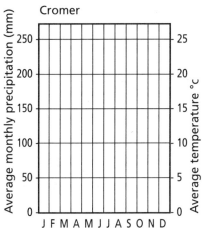

4 Complete the gaps in the following paragraph.

The two coldest months in both Onich and Cromer are _____ and _____. In Plymouth at this time the temperature is ____ degrees warmer. In August the coldest place to be is in _____. One reason why it is relatively cold here is because _____ _____. The lowest annual rainfall is recorded in _____. One reason why it is so low here is because _____. The wettest place throughout the year is _____. One reason why it is so wet here is because _____.

The Green Bridge of Wales

The Green Bridge of Wales (page 55) is a very clear example of a coastal arch. There are several other features that can also be seen on the photograph.

Figure 1 ▶
Sketch of the Green Bridge of Wales, Pembrokeshire

1 Write the following labels alongside the sketch in Figure 1.
   ● arch
   ● layers of rock
   ● stack
   ● high-tide line (the top of the darker staining on the rocks)
   ● cliffs
   ● sea

2 Describe how the arch was formed.

_____

_____

_____

_____

3 You have already labelled a stack on the sketch in Figure 1. Describe how an arch becomes a stack.

_____

_____

_____

_____

4 The Green Bridge of Wales is a popular attraction for visitors to the area. Why do you think it is popular?

_____

_____

Coastal features near Swanage, Dorset
(*part 1*)

The stretch of coast near Swanage in Dorset (Figure 1) is one of the most attractive in the UK. There are dramatic headlands jutting out into the sea separated by wide, sandy bays. The main reason why there are headlands and bays along this stretch of coastline is because there are several different types of rock that outcrop at the coast (Figure 1). The stronger, more resistant rocks do not erode so quickly and, as a result, they form headlands. The weaker, more easily eroded rocks form the bays.

Figure 1 Coastal geology near Swanage, Dorset ▼

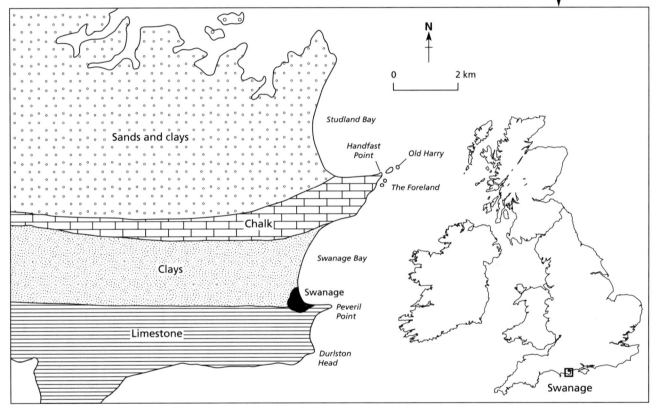

1 What rock forms the headland called The Foreland?

_____

2 Name the other relatively tough rock shown on Figure 1.

_____

3 Explain your answer to Question 2.

_____

_____

4 How resistant to erosion do you think the outcrop of 'sands and clays' is? Explain your answer.

_____

_____

5 Why do you think Swanage is situated in a bay rather than on a headland?

_____

_____

Coastal features near Swanage, Dorset
(*part 2*)

Figure 1 is a sketch of part of The Foreland. It shows some features typical of coastal erosion.

1 Write the following labels in the correct boxes on Figure 1.
- stack
- cave
- joint (crack) in rock
- horizontal layers (beds) of chalk
- arch

2 Describe how Old Harry became separated from the rest of the headland.

_____

_____

_____

_____

_____

_____

▼ *Figure 1 Sketch of part of The Foreland near Swanage, Dorset*

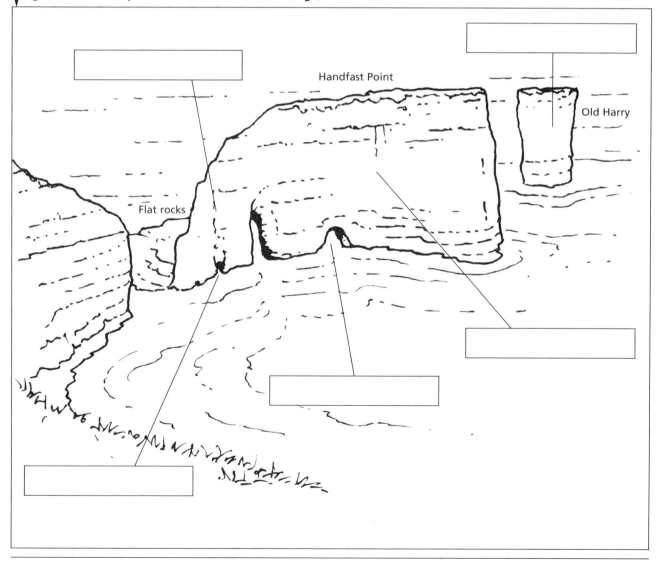

Defending Minehead (*part 1*)

Minehead is a town situated on the north coast of Somerset just to the east of Exmoor (see Atlas Map A, page 9). It has a long history of waterfront activity and used to have a thriving shipyard. Today it still has a busy harbour but it is best known as a seaside resort.

Unfortunately, it has suffered from coastal flooding as a result of particularly high tides, often whipped up by strong winds. Severe flooding in 1996 finally convinced the local authority that a major new coastal defence scheme (Figure 1) needed to be designed.

At a cost of over £12 million a scheme was designed to reduce the wave energy at the seafront and, by building up the beach, reduce the danger of flooding. In addition, access to the beach was made easier for the public and a broad promenade was created for walking alongside the sea wall. The scheme was started in 1997 and finished two years later.

▼ *Figure 1 Minehead beach defences*

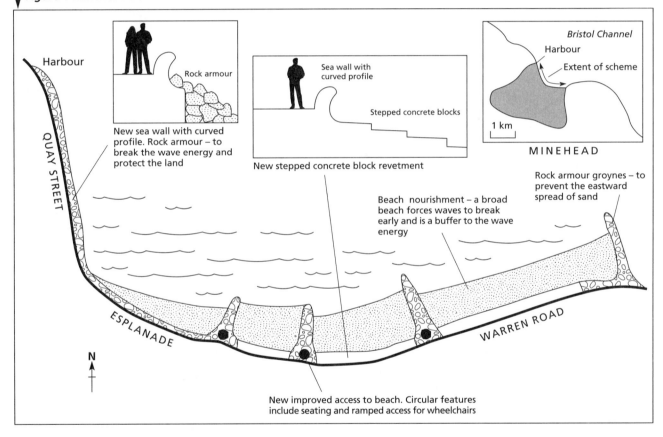

1 Use colours to shade each of the different forms of coastal defence shown in Figure 1.

2 Why was it decided to spend so much money on defending Minehead?

_____

_____

_____

_____

3 What is 'rock armour' and what is its purpose?

_____

_____

_____

_____

_____

Defending Minehead (*part 2*)

▼ *Figure 1 Minehead beach defences*

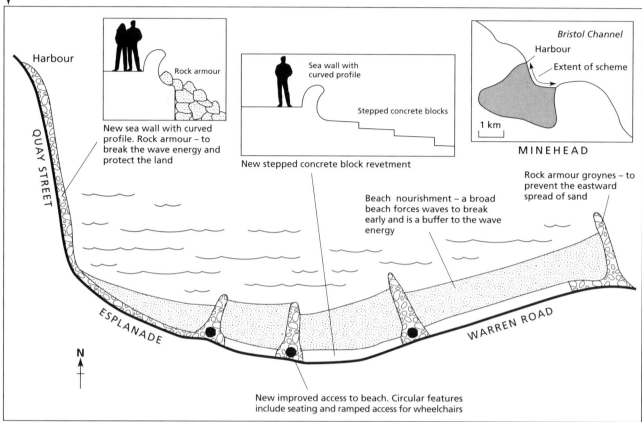

Harbour

QUAY STREET

Rock armour

New sea wall with curved profile. Rock armour – to break the wave energy and protect the land

Sea wall with curved profile

Stepped concrete blocks

New stepped concrete block revetment

Bristol Channel

Harbour

Extent of scheme

1 km

MINEHEAD

Rock armour groynes – to prevent the eastward spread of sand

Beach nourishment – a broad beach forces waves to break early and is a buffer to the wave energy

ESPLANADE

N

WARREN ROAD

New improved access to beach. Circular features include seating and ramped access for wheelchairs

1 Look at the drawing of the sea wall. Why do you think it has a curved face on the seaward side? Draw a sketch to help illustrate your answer.

_____

_____

_____

_____

2 What is the purpose of the rock armour groynes?

_____

_____

_____

3 How has the scheme increased opportunities for local people and tourists to enjoy the seaside?

_____

_____

_____

Retail and leisure parks

In recent years land on the edges of towns and cities has been developed as retail and leisure parks. Large warehouse-type shops selling furniture, DIY products, gardening materials and computers are commonly found alongside ice rinks and multi-screen cinemas. Sometimes old, derelict land is redeveloped and this is usually cheaper than 'greenfield' sites (fields and open countryside). Huge areas of land are developed to cater for the large car parks that are needed for visitors.

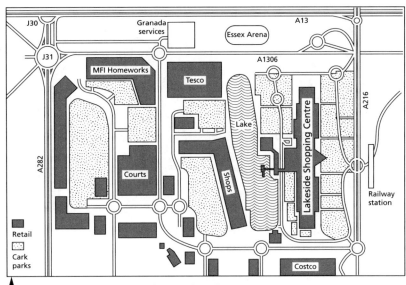

▲ *Figure 1 Map of Lakeside Retail Park*

1 Where is your nearest retail and leisure park?

_____

2 Make a list of some of the shops in the park.

_____ _____

_____ _____

_____ _____

3 What leisure activities are found in the park?

_____ _____

_____ _____

4 How often do you visit your local retail and leisure park, and what do you go there to do?

_____

_____

5 An area of derelict land is called a 'brownfield' site. Why do you think it is given this name?

_____

_____

6 Local people usually prefer a 'brownfield' site to be developed rather than a 'greenfield' site. Why do you think this is so?

_____

_____

_____

_____

7 Suggest two reasons why retail and leisure parks are usually found on the edges of towns and cities.

1 _____

_____

2 _____

_____

Middlebrook retail and leisure park, Bolton

(part 1)

The Middlebrook retail and leisure park occupies a large site to the west of Bolton in north-west England (Figure 1). Work started on the development in the late 1990s, with the centrepiece being the new Reebok Stadium, home of Bolton Wanderers Football Club.

Adjacent to the football stadium is a huge £15 million sports complex consisting of tennis courts, an athletics track and several AstroTurf pitches for all-weather sport. Elsewhere on the site there is a 24-hour multiplex cinema, a bowling alley, several restaurants and a variety of well-known shops including Boots, Alders and Halfords (Figure 1 on Sheet 18).

Industrial premises have also been built, including a Hitachi factory which makes car components. A new railway station has been built for the Reebok Stadium. In total, some 3000 new jobs have been created at the park, which is particularly welcome in a region suffering from high rates of unemployment.

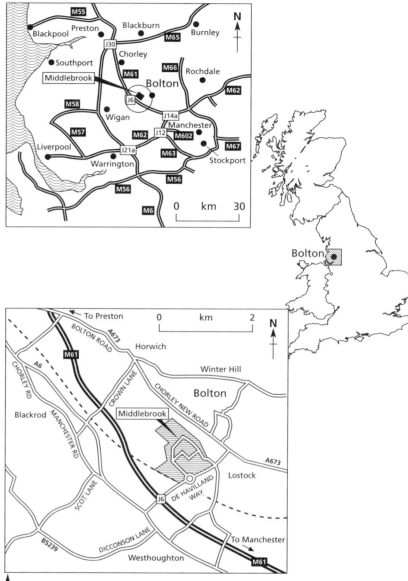

Figure 1 Middlebrook location

Study Figure 1.

1 Near which motorway, and what junction, is Middlebrook located?

Motorway _____

Junction _____

2 Why do you think it is important for Middlebrook to be close to a motorway junction?

_____

_____

3 Describe the motorway route you would take if you wanted to visit Middlebrook from Warrington.

_____

_____

_____

_____

_____

_____

Middlebrook retail and leisure park, Bolton

(part 2)

Study Figure 1.

1 What type of land use occupies the greatest amount of space in the park?

_____

2 Are the retail and leisure shops mixed together or grouped separately?

_____

3 Why do you think the shops have been organised in this way?

_____

_____

4 Describe the position of the petrol station within the park.

_____

5 Why do you think the petrol station is positioned here?

_____

_____

6 Why do you think some of the cafés and restaurants are:

a clustered together in the centre of the leisure outlets?

_____

_____

b located next to roads?

_____

_____

▼ *Figure 1 Plan of Middlebrook retail and leisure park*

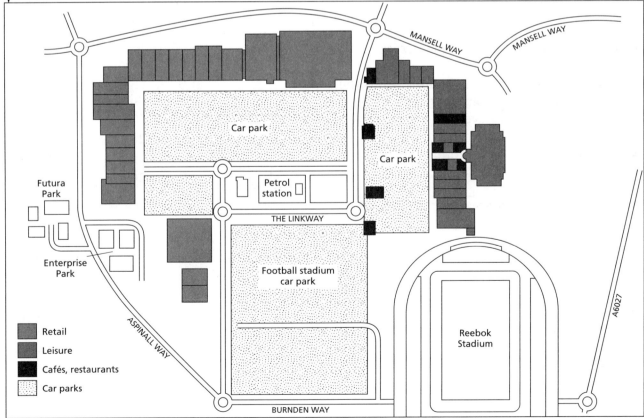

Middlebrook retail and leisure park, Bolton
(part 3)

The management of Middlebrook has carried out vehicle and visitor surveys. Figure 1 presents visitor numbers for each day in April 2000.

Figure 1 Visitors to Middlebrook (April 2000) ▶

Date		Visitors
Sat	1	36,954
Sun	2	24,278
	3	19,782
	4	20,452
	5	20,377
	6	21,232
	7	25,267
Sat	8	32,195
Sun	9	26,571
	10	20,309
	11	21,564
	12	21,068
	13	22,034
	14	25,968
Sat	15	32,933
Sun	16	25,352
H	17	23,152
H	18	25,272
H	19	24,431
H	20	29,370
BH	21	30,054
Sat	22	34,721
Sun	23	13,656
BH	24	27,784
H	25	27,399
H	26	25,596
H	27	25,354
H	28	28,872
Sat	29	32,806
Sun	30	23,693
Total		**768,495**

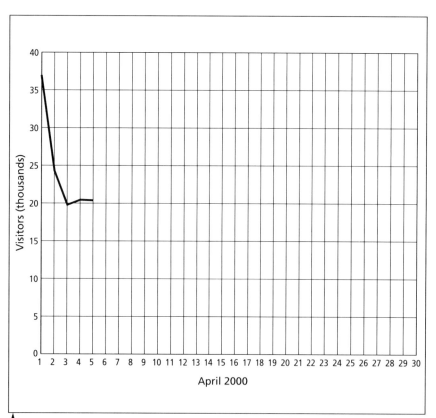

▲ *Figure 2 Visitors to Middlebrook (April 2000)*

1 Plot the information in Figure 1 on to the graph in Figure 2. Join the points with a line. The first five have been done for you.

2 Use a colour to draw a ring around the points for Saturdays.

3 Describe and suggest reasons for the pattern shown by your graph.

H = School Holiday
BH = Bank Holiday

_____

_____

_____

_____

4 Can you think of two reasons why the number of visitors on 23 April was so low?

1 _____

_____

2 _____

_____

Visitors to Northumberland National Park
(part 1)

Northumberland National Park is one of the ten original
National Parks – it is featured as a case study on pages 82/83. In
the 1990s a detailed survey was carried out to discover more
about the visitors to the National Parks. Visitors were asked
where they came from, where they stayed and what they did
during their visit. Some of the data for Northumberland National
Park is given in Table 1 below and on Sheet 21.

1 Look at Table 1. Why do
you think the vast
majority of day visitors
came from the North of
England?

_____

_____

_____

_____

▼ *Table 1 Origin of visitors*

Region	Day %	Holiday %
North of England	92	8
Scotland	4	6
North West of England	2	8
Yorkshire and Humberside	1	14
Wales	–	2
West Midlands	1	7
East Midlands	–	7
South West	–	5
South East and Greater London	–	19
East Anglia	–	5
Northern Ireland	–	1
Overseas (*not to be plotted on Fig. 1*)	–	18

2 Use colours to shade the
map in Figure 1 to show
the pattern of holiday
visitors to
Northumberland
National Park (Table 1).
Complete the key using
the colours suggested.
Notice that the darker
colours indicate the
higher values. Such a
map is called a
'choropleth' map.

3 Why do you think a large
number of holidaymakers
from the South East and
Greater London decided
to visit the Park?

_____

_____

_____

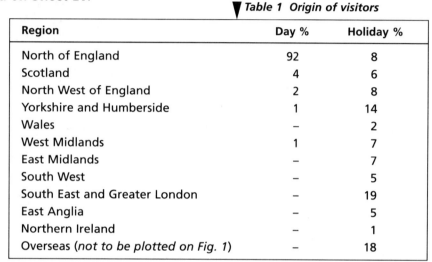

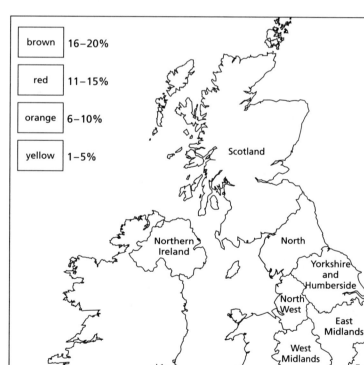

brown 16–20%

red 11–15%

orange 6–10%

yellow 1–5%

Figure 1 Origins of holiday visitors ▶
to Northumberland National Park

Visitors to Northumberland National Park
(part 2)

1 Use the information in Table 1 to complete the pie chart in Figure 1.

2 Why do you think a large number of people staying in the National Park decided to camp or caravan?

_____

_____

3 A lot of people chose to stay in self-catering accommodation. Why is this form of accommodation so popular?

_____

_____

4 The information in Table 2 describes what holiday visitors do in the Park. Use the information to complete the bar chart in Figure 2.

5 Describe the main features of your graph and suggest reasons for the most popular activities.

_____

_____

_____

▼ *Table 1 Where visitors stay*

Accommodation	Percentage	Degrees for pie chart
Hotel	2	7
Bed and breakfast	23	83
Caravan	17	61
Camping	11	40
Self-catering	25	90
Youth hostel	17	61
Others	5	18

▼ *Figure 1 Pie chart – where visitors stay*

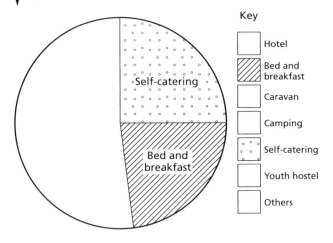

▼ *Table 2 What holiday visitors do*

Activity	Percentage
Sightseeing/driving	89
Picnicking	49
Bird-watching	11
Nature trail	29
Shopping for gifts	46
Visiting a visitor's centre	75
Visiting a historic site	75
Outdoor sports (e.g. rock climbing)	10

Note: The figures add up to over 100 per cent as people often take part in more than one activity.

▼ *Figure 2 Graph to show what holiday visitors do*

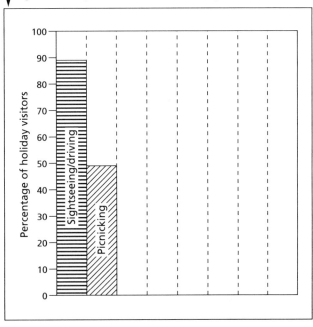

A cornfield food chain

Figure 1 shows some of the plants, animals and birds that live in a cornfield ecosystem. Look carefully at Figure 1 and notice that the diagram is organised in the form of a food chain, starting with the plants at the base of the diagram and finishing with the fox at the top.

1 What is an ecosystem?

_____

2 The cornfield is a natural habitat for many of the creatures in Figure 1. What is another word for 'habitat'?

_____

3 What is a 'food chain'?

_____

4 How many of the creatures in Figure 1 can you identify? Neatly write the names on to Figure 1, using arrows if you wish.

Occasionally, something may happen to wipe out some of the creatures in a food chain: for example, a disease or the use of pesticides. Imagine that the numbers of creatures in Level 3 were dramatically reduced.

5 Describe the likely effects that this reduction would have on the numbers of creatures in Levels 2 and 4, and suggest reasons why.

Effects on Level 2:

_____

_____

_____

Effects on Level 4:

_____

_____

_____

▼ *Figure 1 A cornfield food chain*

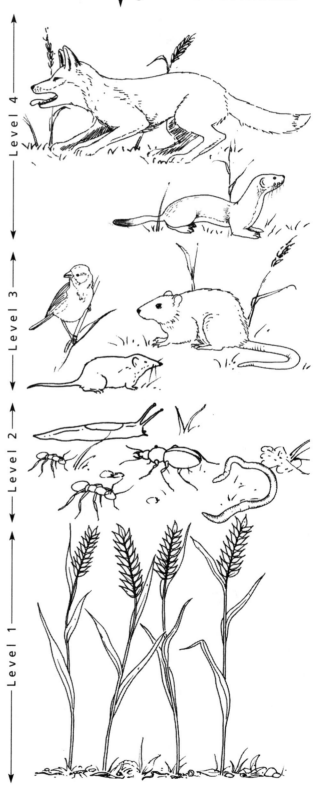

Level 4

Level 3

Level 2

Level 1

The Humberhead Peatlands

The Humberhead Peatlands is an extensive lowland area in Lincolnshire occupying the floodplain of the Humberhead Levels. Over thousands of years a raised bog grew in this wetland environment and the thick peat deposits formed a valuable resource. Peat was first dug hundreds of years ago and used by local people as fuel for fires. In the mid-nineteenth century, it was used as litter for horses and cattle. More recently, it has been used as a compost for farmers and gardeners.

Originally, the peat was dug by hand, but today it is extracted by a machine that works along rows. You can see some of the rows of peat cuttings in Figure 1. Although some peat cutting still takes place to the north of Mill Drain, most of the wetland and old peat cuttings are now managed as a National Nature Reserve by English Nature. Land has been deliberately allowed to flood again in order to restore it to what it used to be like, and many species of birds, plants and animals now thrive in the Reserve.

1 Use the following colours to make Figure 1 easier to understand:
- blue to show the drains (drainage ditches)
- green for the two areas of woodland
- red for the footpaths (the broken line)
- orange for the peat cuttings.

2 The whole area is criss-crossed by drains. Why do you think these were dug in the first place?

_____

3 Describe the pattern of the peat cuttings.

_____

4 Why was peat first dug by local people?

_____

5 Whereabouts on Figure 1 is peat still dug today, and how is it extracted?

_____

6 Why do you think English Nature has encouraged parts of the area to flood again by blocking some of the drains?

_____

_____

_____

_____

7 Why do you think English Nature has left some places inaccessible by public footpath?

_____

_____

_____

_____

_____

Figure 1 The Humberhead Peatlands

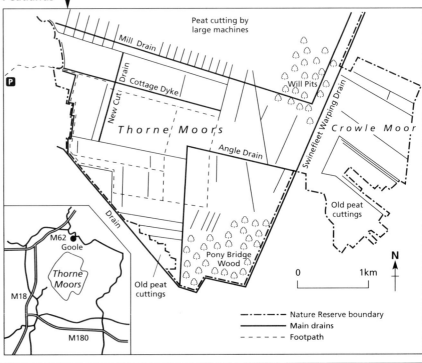

The physical geography of Europe

For the following activities, you will need to refer to Atlas Maps A and B (p.10–11).

1 Which two countries are separated by the:

a Strait of Gibraltar

_____

b Gulf of Bothnia

_____

c Aegean Sea

_____

d St George's Channel

_____

e Skagerrak

_____

2 In which country would you find:

a Lake Vänern and Lake Vättern

_____

b Mount Vesuvius

_____

c River Elbe

_____

d Cape Clear

_____

e Pindus Mountains

_____

3 By how many metres is Mont Blanc higher than the Matterhorn?

_____

4 Which of the following seas is furthest north: Adriatic Sea, Aegean Sea or the Tyrrhenian Sea?

_____

5 Is Iceland north or south of the Arctic Circle?

_____

6 In which two countries would you find the Pennines and the Apennines?

Pennines   _____

Apennines   _____

7 Heads and tails! Draw a line to match up the following river mouths and seas/gulfs:

Rhone	Gulf of Bothnia
Po	Mediterranean Sea
Indals	North Sea
Thames	Gulf of Lions
Ebro	Adriatic Sea

8 Look at Atlas Map B.

a If you travelled north-east from the Orkney Islands, which group of islands would you reach?

_____

b If you then continued your journey in a north-westerly direction, which group of islands would you reach?

_____

c Now travelling due south, which group of islands do you end up on?

_____

Atlas Map A activities

The following activities are based on Atlas Map A (p.10).

1 Is Madrid west or east of London?

_____

2 Is Paris west or east of London?

_____

3 Which of the following cities is furthest north: Stockholm, Oslo or Helsinki?

_____

4 Austria shares its border with how many countries?

_____

5 To which countries do the following islands belong?

a Sardinia _____

b Corsica _____

c The Balearic Islands _____

d Crete _____

e Rhodes _____

6 Between which two countries is Andora?

_____

7 Which European Union capital city is furthest east?

_____

8 Rearrange the following letters to find the German cities

a bmurahg _____

b nobn _____

c krunffrat _____

9 Which of the following pairs of cities is the largest?

a Milan and Venice _____

b Stockholm and Göteborg

_____

c Lyon and Marseille _____

10 What is the straight-line distance between London and Rome? Show your working.

_____

_____

_____

_____

Mapping incomes in the European Union

The 15 countries in the European Union vary a good deal in their wealth as measured by average incomes (Table 1). One method that can be used to plot this information on a map is the choropleth technique (see Skills Box 1, page 9).

▼ *Table 1 European average incomes*

Country	Average income per person (US$)
France	24,990
Germany	27,510
Italy	19,020
Netherlands	24,000
Belgium	24,710
Luxembourg	41,210
UK	18,700
Denmark	29,890
Ireland	14,710
Greece	8,210
Spain	13,580
Portugal	9,740
Austria	26,890
Finland	20,580
Sweden	23,750

1 Complete your choropleth map using the Europe outline on Sheet 27. Use your colours to complete the key boxes, and then carefully colour each country correctly according to the key.

2 Describe the pattern shown by your map. Do incomes vary across the European Union? Is it possible to identify clusters of high-income countries and low-income countries?

_____

_____

_____

3 Suggest some possible reasons why some countries have higher incomes per person than others.

_____

_____

_____

_____

European average incomes

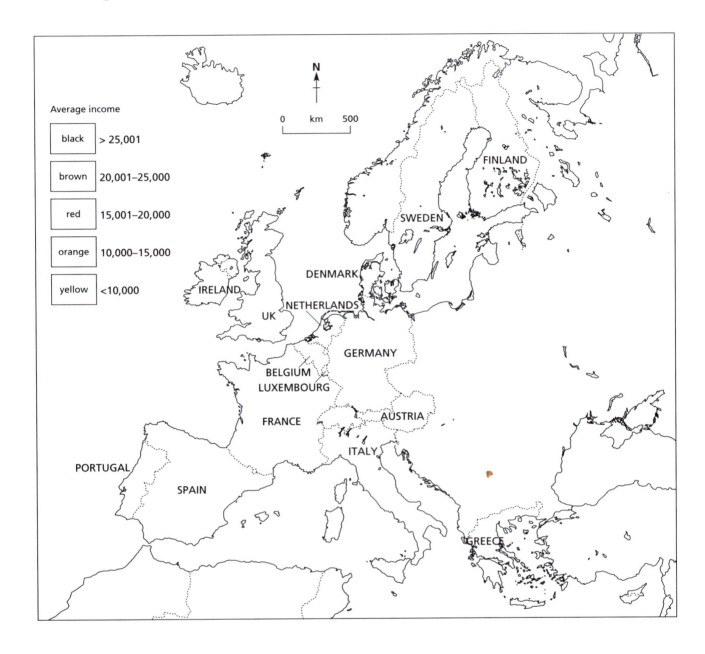

Average income

black	> 25,001
brown	20,001–25,000
red	15,001–20,000
orange	10,000–15,000
yellow	<10,000

Outline map of Europe

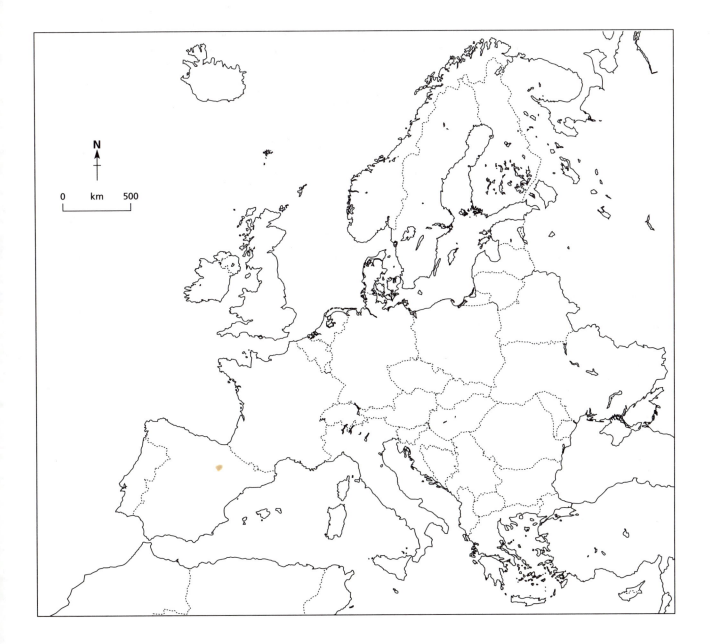

European Union statistics

Country	GDP (ECU per person 1996)	Employment in farming (% 1997)	Employment in industry (% 1997)	Employment in services (% 1997)	Unemployment (% 1997)	Population density (people per km² 1996)	Agricultural area (% of total area 1997)	Crimes (per 100,000 people 1994)
Belgium	20,416	2.7	27.5	69.8	9.2	333	45	5,333
Denmark	20,597	3.8	26.2	70.0	5.5	122	64	10,525
Germany	20,030	2.9	34.7	62.4	10.0	230	49	8,038
Greece	12,326	19.8	22.5	57.7	9.6	80	39	2,956
Spain	13,936	8.3	29.9	61.8	20.8	78	59	2,287
France	18,916	4.6	26.6	68.8	12.4	107	56	6,783
Ireland	16,782	10.9	28.6	60.6	10.1	53	65	2,867
Italy	18,466	6.5	31.7	61.8	12.1	190	56	3,828
Luxembourg	29,440	2.4	23.3	74.3	2.6	161	49	7,384
Netherlands	18,845	3.7	22.9	73.4	5.2	379	44	10,205
Austria	20,400	6.9	29.6	63.5	4.4	96	41	6,314
Portugal	12,656	13.3	31.0	55.7	6.8	108	43	989
Finland	17,375	7.8	27.4	64.8	13.1	15	6	8,028
Sweden	18,140	3.2	25.6	71.2	9.9	22	7	12,620
UK	17,770	1.9	26.9	71.2	7.0	243	66	10,212

(*Source*: European Commission)

See also http://europa.eu.int

Comparing climates: maritime and continental *(part 1)*

Europe's major climate zones are shown in Figure 2.2 (page 15). Apart from the major differences between the north and the south of Europe (as shown by the Enquiry activity, pages 18–19), there are also differences between the Atlantic west coast and the continental interior.

Coastal regions often have a wetter climate than further inland because they are more greatly influenced by the sea. The sea also tends to affect temperatures, giving coastal regions cooler summers but milder winters. This is because water does not heat up or cool down as quickly as land. It retains the heat in the winter but warms only slowly in the summer. An important influence on winter temperatures along the west coast of Europe is the warm North Atlantic Drift ocean current, which keeps the temperatures higher than they would be otherwise.

An area whose climate is greatly influenced by being close to the sea is said to have a 'maritime' climate. An area that is well inland and a long way from the influence of the sea has a 'continental' climate.

Figure 1 shows the location of two places with contrasting climates. Berlin in Germany has a continental climate, whereas Valencia in Ireland has a maritime climate.

▲ *Figure 1 Berlin and Valencia*

1 Use the data in Table 1 on Sheet 31 to construct climate graphs using the axes in Figure 2. Part of the graphs for Berlin and Valencia have already been completed. Draw the climate graph with a pencil first before using colours.

a Shade the precipitation bars in blue.

b Use a red line for the maximum temperature, and blue for the minimum temperature.

2 Use the two graphs to complete the gaps in the following description.

Berlin has much _____ precipitation than Valencia. The total annual precipitation for Berlin is _____ mm compared with _____ mm for Valencia. The wettest season in Berlin is in the _____, whereas the _____ is the wettest time of year in Valencia. The driest month in Valencia is _____ whereas in Berlin it is _____.

Berlin has a much _____ temperature range than Valencia. In July Berlin's maximum temperature averages _____ °C, which is _____ °C higher than the _____ °C recorded in Valencia. Winters in Valencia are quite _____ compared with those in Berlin, where minimum temperatures fall below 0°C in the months of _____, _____, and _____.

3 Why does Valencia have much more rain than Berlin?

_____

_____

4 Why does Berlin have hotter summers and colder winters than Valencia?

_____

_____

Comparing climates: maritime and continental *(part 2)*

5 Suggest one advantage and one disadvantage of the very high precipitation received in Valencia.

Advantage: _____

Disadvantage: _____

6 Suggest one disadvantage of the hot summers and one disadvantage of the cold winters experienced by people living in Berlin.

Summer disadvantage:

_____

Winter disadvantage :

_____

7 In Berlin, much of the summer rainfall occurs in the form of heavy thundery downpours. How does the temperature profile for Berlin help to account for this?

_____

_____

_____

▼ *Figure 2 Climate graphs for Berlin and Valencia*

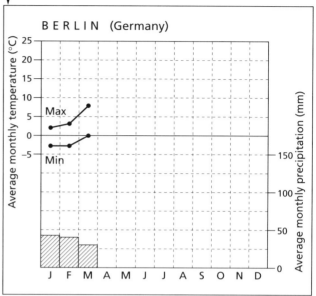

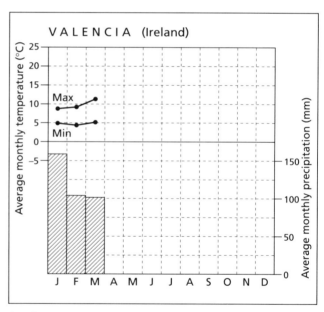

▼ *Table 1 Climate data for Berlin (Germany) and Valencia (Ireland)*

Berlin

Month	Max. Temp. (°C)	Min. Temp. (°C)	Precip. (mm)
J	2	−3	46
F	3	−3	40
M	8	0	33
A	13	4	42
M	19	8	49
J	22	12	65
J	24	14	73
A	23	13	69
S	20	10	48
O	13	6	49
N	7	2	46
D	3	−1	43

Valencia

Month	Max. Temp. (°C)	Min. Temp. (°C)	Precip. (mm)
J	9	5	165
F	9	4	107
M	11	5	103
A	13	6	75
M	15	8	86
J	17	11	81
J	18	12	107
A	18	13	95
S	17	11	122
O	14	9	140
N	12	7	151
D	10	6	168

Mountain climates *(part 1)*

If you have walked to the top of a hill or mountain you will have noticed that it is colder and far more exposed than at lower levels. This explains why few people live high up in mountainous areas. Walkers and climbers have to take special care when venturing into the mountains because the conditions are often harsh and dangerous. They need to be well prepared with plenty of clothes and food, and navigation equipment such as maps and a compass.

When air meets a mountain range it is forced to rise. As it rises it cools and condenses to form clouds and often rain. This type of rainfall is called 'orographic rainfall', and explains why mountains receive high amounts of rainfall. Wind gathers speed at high altitudes because it is not so affected by the friction of the ground. Valleys and canyons may cause the wind to be channelled.

1 Figure 1 explains why mountains often experience high amounts of rainfall.

a Add labels to describe what is happening.

b Give the diagram a title, using the words 'orographic effect'.

2 Why do mountains often experience strong winds?

_____

_____

_____

_____

_____

_____

▼ *Figure 1 Air movement across a mountain range*

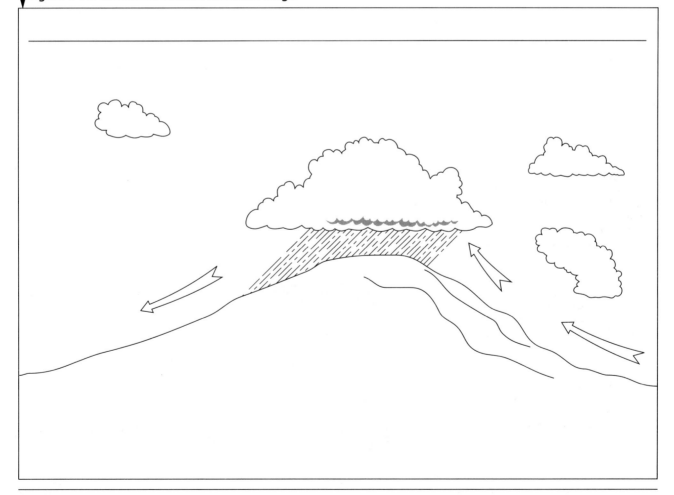

Mountain climates *(part 2)*

1 Figure 2 is a cartoon drawing of a well-dressed fell walker.

a In what ways is she well prepared for the cold?

_____

_____

b In what ways is she well dressed to cope with the wind?

_____

_____

c How is she well prepared for the difficult, often rocky ground?

_____

_____

d She has many useful items in her rucksack. Can you suggest any other items that might prove useful to her?

_____

_____

▼ *Figure 2 What must the well-dressed fell walker wear?*

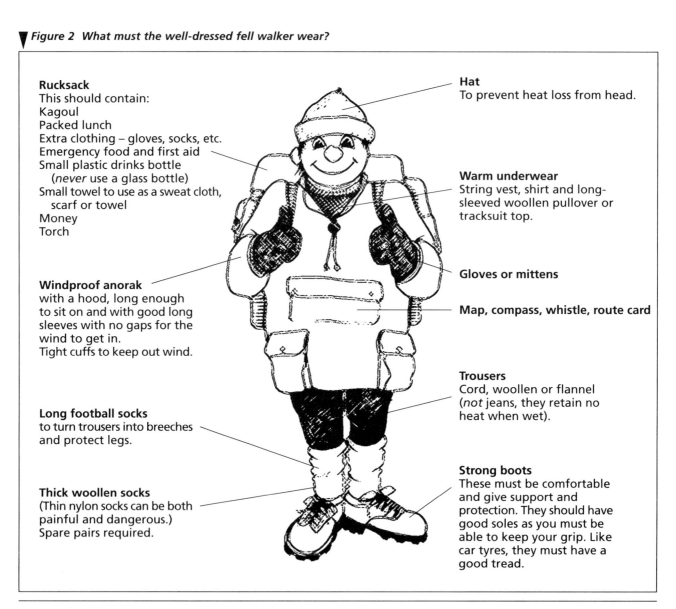

Rucksack
This should contain:
Kagoul
Packed lunch
Extra clothing – gloves, socks, etc.
Emergency food and first aid
Small plastic drinks bottle
   (*never* use a glass bottle)
Small towel to use as a sweat cloth,
   scarf or towel
Money
Torch

Windproof anorak
with a hood, long enough
to sit on and with good long
sleeves with no gaps for the
wind to get in.
Tight cuffs to keep out wind.

Long football socks
to turn trousers into breeches
and protect legs.

Thick woollen socks
(Thin nylon socks can be both
painful and dangerous.)
Spare pairs required.

Hat
To prevent heat loss from head.

Warm underwear
String vest, shirt and long-sleeved woollen pullover or tracksuit top.

Gloves or mittens

Map, compass, whistle, route card

Trousers
Cord, woollen or flannel (*not* jeans, they retain no heat when wet).

Strong boots
These must be comfortable and give support and protection. They should have good soles as you must be able to keep your grip. Like car tyres, they must have a good tread.

Changes to the River Rhine near Freiburg, Germany *(part 1)*

Look closely at the two maps in Figures 1 and 2. They show changes that have taken place to the River Rhine between 1828 and 1963. The area in the maps is generally flat land; it is the river's floodplain.

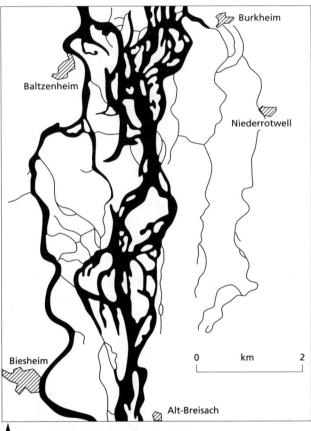

▲ *Figure 1 The River Rhine in 1828*

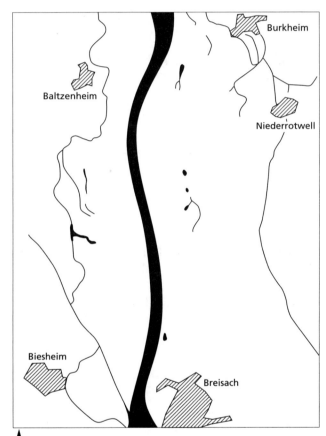

▲ *Figure 2 The River Rhine in 1963*
(Source: ICPR)

Changes to the River Rhine near Freiburg, Germany (part 2)

1 Describe the pattern of river channels in Figure 1.

_____

_____

_____

_____

2 How has the course of the River Rhine changed in Figure 2?

_____

_____

_____

_____

3 How do you think alterations to the River Rhine improved the following?

a Use of the floodplain for farming.

_____

_____

_____

b Travelling between the settlements on the map.

_____

_____

_____

c Navigation of the river by boats.

_____

_____

4 How have the settlements changed between 1828 and 1963?

_____

_____

_____

_____

5 Do you think that flooding would have been more likely in 1828 than in 1963? Explain your answer.

_____

_____

_____

_____

6 a Locate Biesheim on Figure 1 on Sheet 34. What is the name of the river feature here?

_____

b In Figure 2, the river no longer flows close to Biesheim. If you lived in the village, how would you feel about this change?

_____

_____

_____

_____

7 Now that you have studied the two maps in detail, add some labels to the maps to identify the key features and river characteristics.

River restoration: an ICT investigation

Over the years, people have altered river channels to improve drainage of farmland, reduce risks of flooding and improve navigation. While many of these changes have been effective, they have all too often had negative side effects. River courses have become unnatural-looking and less attractive, and wildlife has suffered too. In some cases, the problem of flooding has been made even worse.

Some people have argued that rivers should be allowed to behave naturally and, in recent years, several rivers have, at least in part, been 'restored' to their original courses. This is called 'river restoration'. The European Union has supported a number of demonstration projects, and these are described on the River Restoration Centre's Website at www.qest.demon.co.uk/rrc/rrc/htm.

The following activity can be done either electronically, using a Word document to produce a brochure, with text and annotated photographs, or as a 'cut-and-paste' activity using the Website solely to provide information.

The aim of this activity is to produce a poster or brochure describing the restoration of the River

Skerne in County Durham. Your poster should include the following:

● Location map to show the River Skerne at Darlington, Co. Durham.
● Labelled sketch map to show some of the works carried out.
● Description of the how the river was altered in the first place.
● Description of the restoration works, giving reasons where possible.
● How you think the scheme has benefited the local people.

1 Access the River Restoration Centre's Website and click 'Demonstration Projects'.

2 Click 'River Skerne'.

3 Scroll through the information, taking time to study the sketch map and the photographs. One of the photographs is an aerial shot, which could be transferred to a Word document to be cropped and labelled.

4 A simplified outline sketch of the project and a sketch of the aerial photograph are given here if you wish to make use of them.

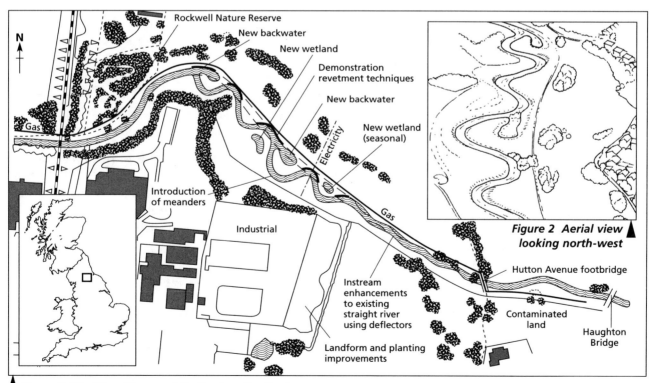

Rockwell Nature Reserve
New backwater
New wetland
Demonstration revetment techniques
New backwater
New wetland (seasonal)
Electricity
Introduction of meanders
Industrial
Gas
Instream enhancements to existing straight river using deflectors
Landform and planting improvements
Contaminated land
Hutton Avenue footbridge
Haughton Bridge

Figure 2 Aerial view looking north-west

▲ *Figure 1 The River Skerne at Darlington, Co. Durham*
(Source: River Restoration Centre)

Aviaries Farm case study: an update using ICT *(part 1)*

Aviaries Farm is one of several UK case studies featured on the National Farmers' Union's Website. The details are regularly updated and allow you to compare recent data with that contained in your textbook. The aim of this investigation is to find the most recent information about the farm and to see how things have changed in recent years.

Access the NFU site at www.nfu.org.uk.

Click 'Education'.

Click 'Farm studies'.

Scroll down to 'Organic dairy and arable' and click to open.

1 Complete the table below to show the land use at Aviaries Farm for the latest date available.

▼ *Table 1 Land Use at Aviaries Farm*

Type	Crop	1997 (hectares)	
Arable	Winter wheat	100	
	Spring wheat	16.6	
	Spring oats	0	
	Triticale	8.9	
	Potatoes	17	
	Swedes (for human consumption)	10.9	
	Sweetcorn	0.9	
	Arable total	154.3	
Fodder crops	Turnips	3	
	Kale	12.1	
	Fodder beet	12.1	
	Grass ley	206.2	
	Fodder crop total	233.4	
Grass keep		28	
Woodland, tracks etc.		21	
Set-aside	Grass ley	8.6	
	Woodland	2.1	
	Other	0.4	
	Set-aside total	11.1	
Farm total (including other categaries)		510.1	

2 Describe some of the major changes that have taken place in land use.

_____

_____

_____

_____

_____

_____

_____

_____

_____

_____

_____

3 Use the 'hot links' or 'Glossary' to look up the following types of land use:
- triticale

_____

- fodder beet

_____

- grass ley

_____

Aviaries Farm case study *(part 2)*

4 Read through the information in the farm study (see Sheet 37) to find out what farm machinery has been purchased since 1997 and how much it cost.

_____

_____

_____

_____

5 Use the 'hot link' to find out more about land set-aside.

_____

_____

_____

6 Why are rabbits, badgers and birds of prey a problem for Mr Dowding?

• rabbits _____

_____

• badgers _____

_____

• birds of prey _____

_____

7 Use the information available on the Web page to complete a farm systems diagram showing inputs, processes and outputs. Write the information in the diagram in Figure 1, and use some drawings to make it look more attractive.

▼ *Figure 1 Inputs, processes and outputs at Aviaries Farm*

Inputs	Processes (farm activities)	Outputs

Farming changes

Look at the drawings in Figures 1. They show how the farming
landscape of the United Kingdom has changed over the years.

▼ *Figure 1 Farming changes in the UK*

 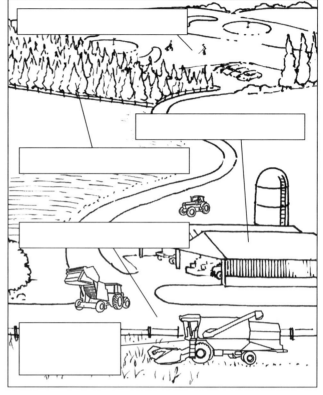

1 Write the following labels in the correct
boxes on Figure 1.
- Small fields with hedgerows.
- Modern combine harvester.
- Large farm sheds for storage.
- Collection of small farm buildings and
  cottages.
- Horses used for ploughing.
- Main road serving the farm.
- Farmland now used as a golf course.
- Fields planted with conifer trees.

2 Why do you think that farmers have made
their fields larger?

_____

_____

3 How might the removal of hedgerows
affect wildlife?

_____

_____

4 In the 1930s most farms kept horses.
Why?

_____

5 Over the years, fewer people have been
employed as farm workers. Why do you
think this is so?

_____

6 Why have some farmers started to use
their land for other purposes, e.g. golf
courses?

_____

_____

_____

_____

_____

Oranges: an example of Mediterranean farming *(part 1)*

One of the main types of farming in Europe is Mediterranean farming. This involves growing crops that are ideally suited to the hot and dry summers and mild but wet winters that are associated with a Mediterranean climate. A range of crops is grown including grapes, olives, tomatoes and citrus fruit such as oranges, lemons and limes.

Oranges are well suited to Mediterranean conditions. The climate provides the orange trees with the warmth and long hours of sunshine needed to ripen the fruit, and the mild winters enable harvesting to take place over several months. In addition, the trees are well suited to surviving in the dry conditions (see Figure 3.2, page 18). However, during very dry summers, irrigation is needed and this is supplied from nearby rivers and from underground boreholes.

1 Study Figure 3.2 (page 18) to remind yourself how the orange tree is well adapted to survive the hot and dry Mediterranean summers.

2 Write a couple of sentences saying why oranges are ideally suited to be grown in the Mediterranean region.

_____

_____

_____

_____

3 One of the main regions for producing oranges and other citrus fruit is Valencia in Spain. Some 50 per cent of Spanish oranges are grown there.

a Use the data in Table 1 to complete the graph in Figure 1.

b Describe the changes in citrus production between 1991 and 1996.

_____

_____

_____

Table 1 Production of selected citrus fruit in Valencia province, Spain (tonnes) ▼

Citrus fruit	1991	1996
Oranges	105,600	78,190
Mandarins	27,800	41,270
Lemons	245,850	214,970

Figure 1 Production of selected citrus fruits in Valencia, Spain ▼

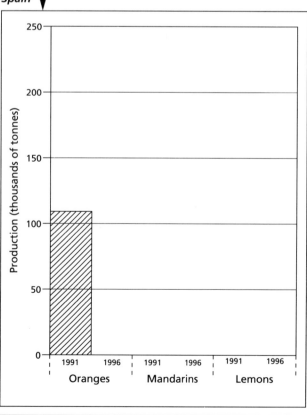

Oranges: an example of Mediterranean farming *(part 2)*

1 Table 1 lists the production of oranges in European countries in 1995.

a Draw a choropleth map to show this information, using the colours suggested in Figure 1.

b Write a few sentences describing and trying to explain the pattern of orange production in the European Union.

_____

_____

_____

_____

2 Try to discover the answers to the following questions:

a What type of orange is used for making marmalade?

_____

b What are satsumas and what time of year do we usually find them in shops?

_____

c Which citrus fruit is often squeezed over pancakes?

_____

d Another citrus fruit grown in the Valencia area is the 'pomelo'. What is the English name for this fruit?

_____

Table 1 Production of oranges in European Union countries (1995) ▼

Country	Production (tonnes)
Greece	935,000
Italy	1,597,000
Portugal	209,000
Spain	2,435,000

▼ **Figure 1 Production of oranges in the European Union**

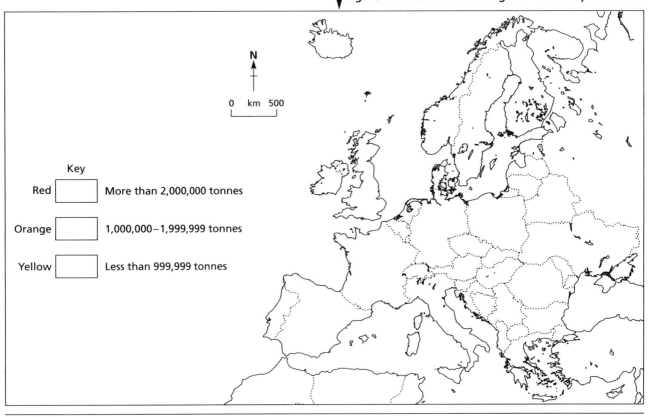

Key

Red ☐ More than 2,000,000 tonnes

Orange ☐ 1,000,000–1,999,999 tonnes

Yellow ☐ Less than 999,999 tonnes

The farmer's year, Aviaries Farm

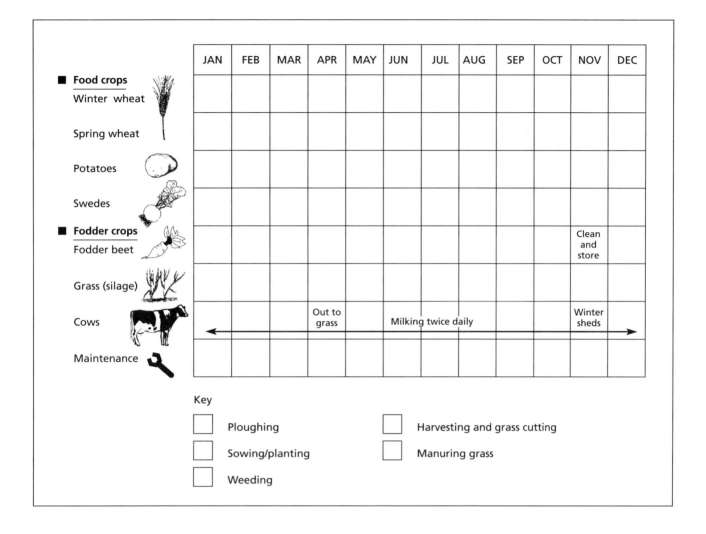

	JAN	FEB	MAR	APR	MAY	JUN	JUL	AUG	SEP	OCT	NOV	DEC
■ **Food crops** / Winter wheat												
Spring wheat												
Potatoes												
Swedes												
■ **Fodder crops** / Fodder beet											Clean and store	
Grass (silage)												
Cows			← Out to grass			Milking twice daily					Winter sheds →	
Maintenance												

Key

☐ Ploughing   ☐ Harvesting and grass cutting

☐ Sowing/planting   ☐ Manuring grass

☐ Weeding

Plan of Cherry Tree Farm

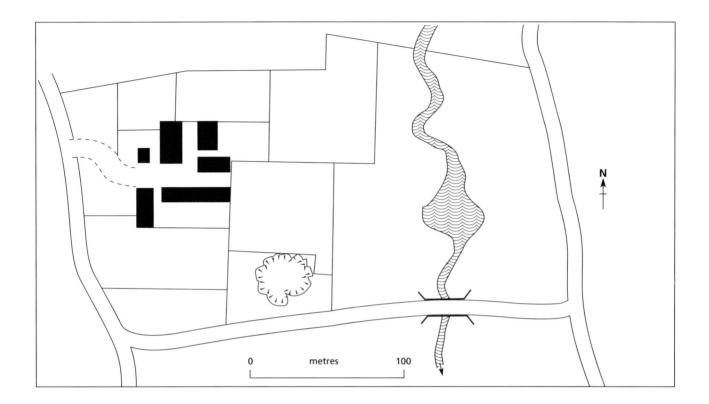

N

0   metres   100

Wind power: an ICT investigation

The aim of this investigation is for you to find out more about wind power by using a Danish Website.

Access www.windpower.dk

Scroll down to see the different Web pages available at this site. In order to answer the questions that follow, you will have to 'surf' the various pages to find out where the information lies. You may find information on more than one Web page (for a start, click 'FAQs').

1   Some people think wind turbines are noisy. Try to find out more about this issue.

_____

_____

2   Is wind energy expensive?

_____

_____

3   Can wind turbines be sited absolutely anywhere?

_____

_____

4   Try to find out whether wind turbines have any harmful effects on wildlife.

_____

_____

_____

5   Some people think that wind turbines spoil the landscape, while others think that they add beauty and interest. Within the 'Guided Tour' section, you will find out more about this issue. What do you think and why?

_____

_____

_____

Glacial landscapes

Figure 1 is a sketch of part of the Lake District in England. The area has been covered by ice in the past, and much of the present landscape is the result of glacial erosion.

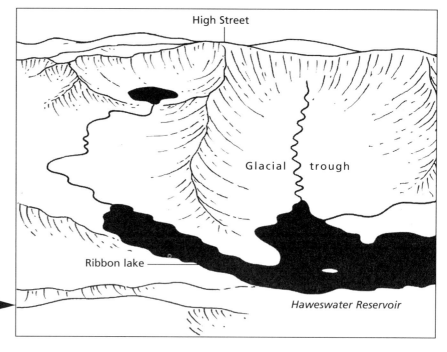

High Street

Glacial trough

Ribbon lake

Haweswater Reservoir

Figure 1 Sketch of a glaciated landscape at High Street, Lake District

1 Draw arrows on the rivers in Figure 1 to show in which direction they are flowing.

2 A glacial trough has been labelled on Figure 1. Describe the valley floor and sides.

Valley floor: _____

_____

Valley sides: _____

_____

3 Label the following features:
● a corrie;
● a tarn (corrie lake).

4 An arête is a knife-edged ridge that separates two valleys or two corries. It is a common feature in glaciated areas.

a Label an arête on Figure 1.

b Footpaths often follow arêtes. Why do you think this is?

_____

c How would you feel about walking along an arête footpath?

_____

5 A feature called a ribbon lake is labelled on Figure 1. Why do you think it is called this?

_____

_____

6 Suggest why there are few roads and settlements in this part of the Lake District.

_____

_____

_____

_____

_____

_____

Avalanches: an ICT investigation

The aim of this investigation is for you to find out about recent avalanche incidents that have occurred in Europe.

1 Access the Cyberspace Avalanche Center at http://www.csac.org/Incidents.

2 Scroll through the table of recent avalanches and complete Table 1 below, listing details of ten recent European avalanches. It is up to you which ones to include in your table. You could concentrate on a single country, try to get a spread of countries, or list those where fatalities occurred.

▼ *Table 1 Recent European avalanches*

Date	Location	Fatalities	Activity

3 Choose one of the incidents and click 'Report' to find out more about the incident. Write your own report about the incident in the box alongside in the style of a newspaper article. Add diagrams and pictures if you wish (you could search the Internet for a good photo), and don't forget to make up a headline.

Spanish wetlands under threat *(part 1)*

The Doñana area of southern Spain (see Figure 1) is one of the most important wetland sites in Europe. It has been designated a Natural World Heritage Site and is internationally recognised as a Biosphere Reserve.

The low-lying, marshy landscape, with its many rivers, lagoons and sand dunes, is home to many species of birds and is a particularly important wintering ground for ducks. There are also many other rare species including vipers, eagles, wildcat, boar and the endangered Spanish lynx.

The area has been under threat from urban development, the extraction of water for irrigation, poaching and, most recently, from water pollution. In April 1998, the area was threatened by toxic waste from a mine. Read the newspaper extract in Figure 2 to see what happened.

The emergency measures that were taken to prevent the flow entering the park seems to have been successful, but there may still be problems resulting from the pollution of the surrounding farmland and the underground water. These effects have still to be assessed.

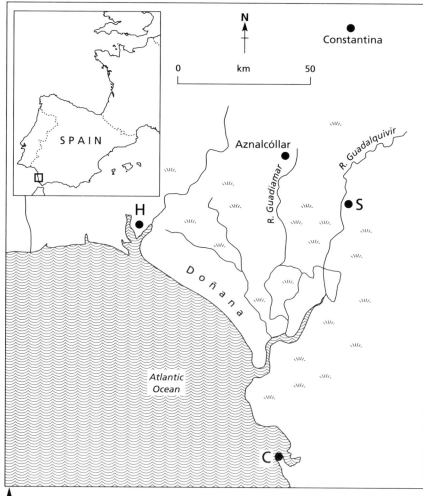

▲ *Figure 1 The Doñana wetlands, Spain*

▼ *Figure 2 Newspaper extract*

The Spanish authorities are fighting around the clock to contain what the government called 'an ecological disaster of major proportions' after a torrent of toxic mining waste gushed into the river skirting Spain's most important natural reserve.

The Guadiamar river rose two metres above its normal level under the impact of the deadly effluent (a wave of black sludge laden with cyanide, arsenic and lead) that burst from a 50-metre gash in the mine reservoir's cement walls. Up to 6000 hectares of farmland along the river's banks were inundated by the toxic black mud as it made its journey to the sea. There were fears that high tides sluicing up-river could force the poisons into the soil, causing long-term damage to the area.

Government officials insisted that emergency shoring-up operations at the weekend had diverted the spill and saved the wetlands – but only time would tell.

(*Source: Independent*, 27 April 1998)

Spanish wetlands under threat *(part 2)*

1   Use Atlas Map C (page 83) to label the three towns H, S and C on Figure 1 on Sheet 47.

2   Locate the Doñana area on Atlas Map C and describe the physical features of the area.

_____

_____

_____

3   Why is the Doñana area so special?

_____

_____

_____

4   What was the source of pollution in April 1998?

_____

5   How might the pollution have long-term effects on the area?

_____

_____

_____

6   Describe how the authorities saved the Doñana Reserve.

_____

_____

_____

7   Find out more about the Doñana wetlands by accessing the World Conservation Monitoring Centre at www.wcmc.org.uk/protected_areas/data/wh/donana.html or the UNESCO site at www.unesco.org/whc/sites/685.htm. Try to discover more about what is so special about the Reserve and what have been the recent threats, apart from the pollution incident of 1998.

General geography of Spain

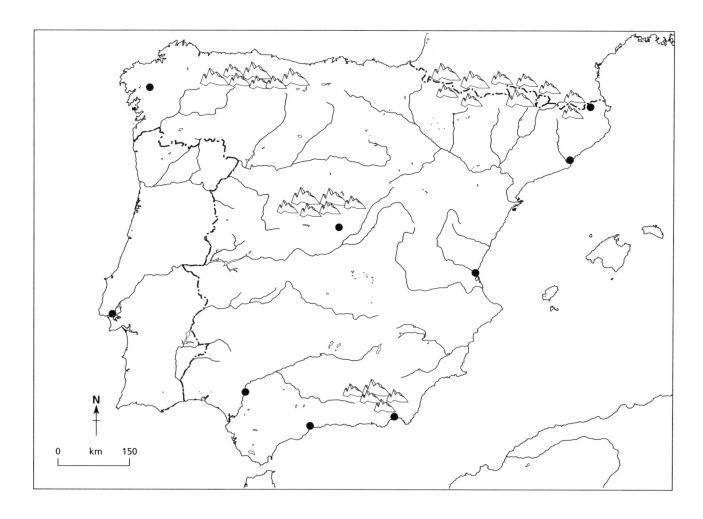

Visiting the Camargue: an ICT activity

The aim of this activity is to produce a single-sided tourist leaflet describing the attractions and opportunities available to visitors to the Camargue Regional Nature Park.

Your brief

To produce an attractive and informative single-sided sheet aimed to encourage visitors to the Camargue. It should describe the main attractions of the Camargue, suggest places of interest and concentrate particularly on the flamingos. The leaflet should be attractively designed and look appealing.

The leaflet should be produced electronically: for example, as a Word document. If possible, you should try to make use of the 'draw' facilities and the importing of photographs from the Internet (which you can 'crop' and 'text wrap' if you wish).

Resources

1 Your textbook (pages 103–7) will provide you with some background information.

2 The Camargue Regional Nature Park maintains a Website at

http://www.parcs-naturels-regionaux.tm.fr/lesparcs/camaa_en.html

(if you have problems connecting, try www.parcs-naturels-reionaux.tm.fr and click 'Les 38 Parcs', then click 'English'.

3 Conduct a search for more information, using a search engine such as Yahoo, or use CD-ROM encyclopedias such as Encarta.

Parc naturel régional de Camargue

Français

The Camargue Regional Nature Park

Grande Camargue (750 km2), located at the mouth of the Rhone River, extends across the entire river delta area. Different from the Petite Camargue, or Camargue Gardoise, located West of the Little Rhone, it is often said to be an "island," because cut off by the Mediterranean and two arms of the Rhone River. The Rhone Delta drifted periodically until the end of the 19th century. These geological and geophysical characteristics have made this vast expanse what it is today, the result of successive sedimentation from the ebb and flow of the river and the sea.

Outline map of France

N

0   km   150

Hydroelectricity in Sweden *(part 1)*

Hydroelectricity involves generating electricity from the power of moving water. It is an example of a renewable power source. A hydroelectric power plant is usually sited on a fast-flowing stretch of water. A dam is built and water is then released through tunnels to drive the huge turbines that generate the electricity (see Figure 1). The electricity is then transmitted around the country via the national grid.

Sweden has an abundance of hydroelectric resources, and it was the harnessing of this form of energy that led to the development of industries such as pulp and paper, iron and steel, and the smelting of copper, silver and other metals. Hydroelectricity, together with nuclear power, accounts for approximately 90 per cent of Sweden's electricity production.

The bulk of the hydropower is produced along nine rivers in the north of Sweden. The most productive river is the River Lule, with fifteen

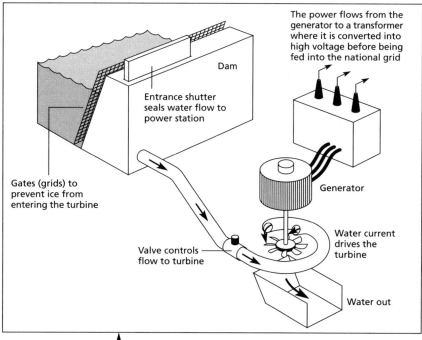

▲ Figure 1 Generating hydroelectricity

power stations. Other important rivers include the Ume and the Indals. In the interest of preserving untouched nature the Government has decided to protect some rivers, including the Vindel, the Kalix and the Torne, from development.

---

1 What is hydroelectricity?

_____

2 Why is hydroelectricity an example of a renewable form of energy?

_____

_____

3 Study Figure 1.

a Why do you think there are grids to prevent ice from entering the turbine?

_____

b Why is it necessary to build a dam?

_____

c The water rushing out below the power station is very fast-flowing. What dangers might this present downstream?

_____

_____

_____

4 How has the development of hydroelectricity helped Sweden's economy to grow?

_____

_____

_____

Hydroelectricity in Sweden (part 2)

For this activity you will need to refer to Atlas Map E (page110).

1 Complete the map in Figure 1 to show some of the characteristics of hydroelectricity production in Sweden.

a Draw the extent of the high ground in Sweden (land over 500 m) and shade it with a colour.

b Identify the three main rivers where hydroelectricity is produced and shade them red.

c Identify the three protected rivers and shade them green.

d Name the rivers, the towns and the surrounding seas.

e Give your map a title and explain the colours in a key.

2 Why is most of Sweden's hydroelectricity produced in the north?

_____

_____

_____

_____

_____

_____

_____

_____

_____

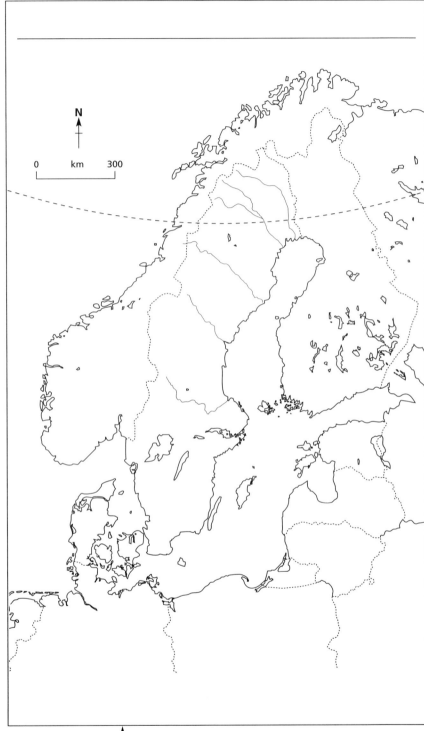

▲ *Figure 1 Outline map of Sweden*

Farming in Sweden (part 1)

Read the following extract from a factsheet about Swedish farming written by the Swedish Institute.

Sweden is one of the largest countries in Europe. About half of the land area is covered by forest. Over a third of the country is mountains, lakes and marshes. Less than a tenth of Sweden's total area – slightly under 3 million ha – is under cultivation.

Sweden has a relatively favourable climate, considering its northern position. The scope for agriculture, however, varies a great deal between the north and south of the country. The growing period in the extreme south is 240 days, while in the far north it is below 120. The climate of central and southern Sweden can be termed temperate. Annual precipitation averages about 600 mm.

Agriculture, along with forestry, hunting and fishing, provides employment for only a minor part of the Swedish population. Most farms are family concerns, in which most of the work is done by the members of the family. Part-time farming, with income supplemented by other employment, has become a common feature in agriculture. To many farms this means economic stability and all-year-round employment. In the densely forested parts of Sweden, farming is often combined with forestry, and roughly 73 per cent of Swedish agricultural enterprises are engaged in this kind of combination farming.

The last 40 years have seen a reduction in the number, but increase in the size, of agricultural enterprises. Farmers have invested great sums in machinery and equipment, while at the same time specialising in grain, milk production or pig rearing. Smaller farms are mostly located in the northern parts of the country and in densely forested areas, while large farms are generally located in the flat areas of the south.

Production

Arable farming

Some 43 per cent of the arable land is used for grain, mostly barley, wheat and oats. The differing climatic conditions in different parts of the country affect the choice of crops grown. Ley, green fodder and feed grain are the main crops cultivated in the north. The production of cereals is concentrated in the flat lands of central and southern Sweden. Oilseed rape cultivation also takes place mainly in the southern and central regions of the country. Potatoes are grown everywhere, but sugar beet is grown mainly in the southernmost part of Sweden.

Horticulture

The commercial production of vegetables, fruit and berries, as well as ornamental and nursery plants, is carried out both indoors and out, mainly in the more southerly regions of the country. During the 1980s, however, there was an increase in horticulture even further north, and in 1996 there were approximately 4100 horticultural enterprises in the country as a whole.

Products of animal origin

There are roughly 1.8 million head of cattle in Sweden, including slightly less than 470,000 dairy cows which produce more than 3 million tonnes of milk annually. A restructuring of milk production during the past ten years has meant that the number of dairy herds has been cut by almost half, and the total number of dairy cows has been reduced by more than 25 per cent. The decline in the total milk production has opened the way for increased beef cattle rearing.

Pig farming, and the production of eggs and poultry, is also a sizeable industry in Sweden, though the production of mutton and lamb is relatively limited.

1 What percentage of land in Sweden can be cultivated?

_____

2 Why is southern Sweden better suited for cereal crops than the north?

_____

_____

_____

3 What is meant by 'combination farming' and why is it popular?

_____

_____

_____

_____

Farming in Sweden *(part 2)*

1

a Present the data in Table 1 as a line graph, using the axes in Figure 1.

Table 1 Number of farming enterprises in Sweden, 1951–96 ▼

1951	282,187
1961	232,920
1971	150,014
1981	115,136
1991	93,554
1996	90,488

(Source: Statistics Sweden)

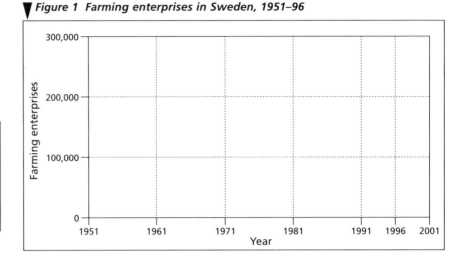

▼ *Figure 1 Farming enterprises in Sweden, 1951–96*

b Suggest possible reasons for the reduction in the number of farming enterprises.

_____

_____

▼ ***Table 2 Arable land utilisation, 1996***

	%
Cereals	13
Feed grains	30
Ley/green fodder	36
Potatoes/sugar beet	3
Oil plants	3
Legumes, misc. plants	3
Fallow, uncultivated land	12

(Source: Statistics Sweden)

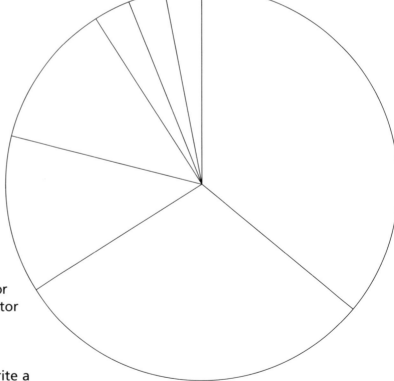

2 Present the information in Table 2 in the form of a pie chart. The chart has already been drawn for you in Figure 2 but you will need to use a protractor to discover which sector is which. Use colours for each sector and explain them in a key.

3 Use the information above to write a summary of Swedish farming in the form of a poster. You could use labels to show differences between the south and the north. Use colours and illustrations to make your diagram more attractive. An alternative would be to produce your summary diagram electronically as a Word document, allowing you to make use of 'draw' facilities, 'clip-art', and so on.

Outline map of Sweden

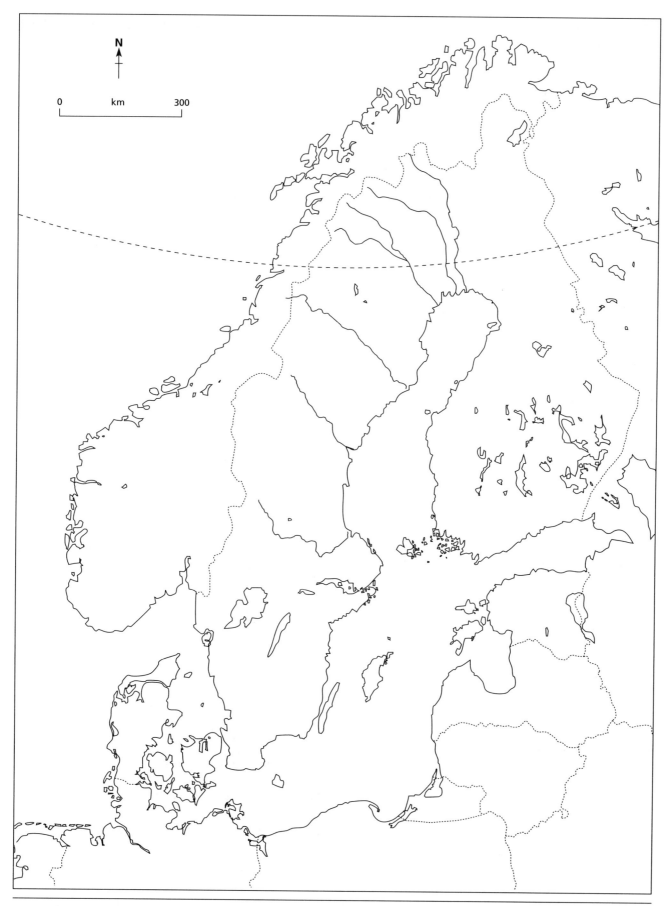

Atlas map activities *(part 1)*

The following activities refer to Atlas Maps A and B (pages 10–11, 12–13).

1 In which continent are the following mountain ranges located?

a Andes _____

b Himalaya _____

c Rocky Mountains _____

d Atlas Mountains _____

e Alps _____

2 In which oceans would you find the following island groups?

a Galapagos _____

b Maldives _____

c Canary _____

d Marshall _____

e Cape Verde _____

3 What is the name of the desert that is found along the border of India and Pakistan?

_____

4 Which African desert is found on the tropic of Capricorn?

_____

5 What is the name and height above sea level of North America's highest mountain?

_____

6 Which pairs of countries are separated by the:

a Tasman Sea

_____

b Sea of Japan

_____

c South China Sea

_____

d Mozambique Channel

_____

e Davis Strait

_____

7 Match the following capital cities and countries:

Ulan Bator	Cuba
Ankara	Australia
Dodoma	Finland
Canberra	Taiwan
Taibei	Mongolia
Helsinki	Morocco
Addis Ababa	Turkey
Bogotá	Tanzania
Havana	Colombia
Rabat	Ethiopia

8 Which of the following countries in each pair is further north?

a Sri Lanka and Cuba _____

b Uruguay and Paraguay _____

c Papua New Guinea and Zambia

_____

Atlas map activities *(part 2)*

9 Complete the spaces in the following alphabet:

River in Brazil

A _____

Capital of China

B _____

Mountain range between the Black Sea and the Caspian Sea

C _____

Country whose capital is Copenhagen

D _____

Continent   E _____

Russian? F _____

Country mostly covered by ice

G _____

Canadian bay

H _____

Large southern Asian country

I _____

Tokyo is its capital city

J _____

Country split into North and South

K _____

Turkana in Kenya is an example

L _____

Country whose capital is Kuala Lumpur

M _____

Country separating China from India

N _____

The Indian is one of several examples

O _____

The largest 'O' in the world

P _____

Small country in the Middle East

Q _____

The 'Great Barrier' is an example

R _____

Northern region in the Russian Federation

S _____

Southerly point in South America

T _____

South American country

U _____

South American country

V _____

Capital of New Zealand

W _____

Town in China

X _____

River flowing into the Arctic Ocean

Y _____

River flowing through Mozambique

Z _____

Testing relationships using Spearman's Rank Correlation Test *(part 1)*

Worked example

In this example, we shall examine the relationship between wealth (GNP) and birth rates. One might expect birth rates to be lowest in richer countries. Let's see.

▼ *Table 1 Wealth and birth rate statistics*

Country	GNP $ per person, 1998	Rank of GNP	Birth rate (per 1000) 1997	Rank of birth rate	Difference between ranks (d)	Difference squared (d²)
Bangladesh	350	8	28	4	4	16
Brazil	4,570	4	21	7	3	9
China	750	7	17	8	1	1
Iran	1,770	6	22	6	0	0
Mexico	3,970	5	25	5	0	0
Nigeria	300	9	40	2	7	49
Saudi Arabia	7,040	3	35	3	0	0
Tanzania	210	10	41	1	9	81
UK	21,400	2	12	10	8	64
USA	29,340	1	15	9	8	64

- Rank each country in descending order (highest value ranked 1, and so on) for both sets of data.
- Work out the difference (d) between the two ranks for each country.
- Square the difference (d^2).
- Add up the squares of the differences to give Σd^2 (Σ means 'the sum of').
- Insert the values into the formula:

$$R = 1 - \left(\frac{6 \times \Sigma d^2}{n^3 - n} \right)$$

Where n = number of countries.
$\Sigma d^2 = 284$
$R = 1 - (6 \times 284) / (1000 - 10)$
$R = 1 - 1704 / 990$
$R = 1 - 1.72$
$R = -0.72$
The value of R will lie between -1 and $+1$. A negative R indicates a negative relationship (as one value increases the other decreases) and a positive R indicates a positive relationship (as one value increases, so does the other).

What does the result mean?
- The closer the R value is to -1 or $+1$, the stronger the relationship.
- -1 or $+1$ indicates a perfect relationship.
- Values between + or $- 0.7$ and + or $- 1$ indicate a good relationship, increasing in strength towards + or -1.

   The example above suggests a *good negative relationship* between birth rate and wealth.

Testing relationships using Spearman's Rank Correlation Test *(part 2)*

In this activity you will be making use of some population data. The main aim of this activity is to see whether there is any relationship between wealth (GNP) and life expectancy.

There are several ways to compare sets of data to see how well they are related. You have already come across scattergraphs, for example. We are going to use a simple statistical test called Spearman's Rank Correlation Test to examine the relationship between wealth and

life expectancy. In theory, we would expect life expectancy to be highest in wealthy countries – we shall see!

First of all, follow through the worked example on Sheet 59 to see how the test works.

Now use the Spearman's Rank Correlation Test to examine the strength of the relationship between wealth (GNP) and life expectancy.

1 Complete the columns in Table 1. Two countries have been done for you.

▼ *Table 1 Wealth and life expectancy statistics*

Country	GNP $ per person, 1998	Rank of GNP	Life expectancy (years), 1997	Rank of life expectancy	Difference between ranks (*d*)	Difference squared (*d²*)
Bangladesh	350	8	58			
Brazil	4,570	4	67			
China	750	7	70			
Iran	1,770	6	69			
Mexico	3,970	5	72			
Nigeria	300	9	54			
Saudi Arabia	7,040	3	71			
Tanzania	210	10	48			
UK	21,400	2	77	1	1	1
USA	29,340	1	76	2	1	1

2 Now apply the Spearman's Rank Test, showing all your working.

$$R = 1 - \left(\frac{6 \times \Sigma d^2}{n^3 - n} \right)$$

Where $n = 10$

_____

_____

_____

_____

_____

3 What is your *R* value?

_____

4 What does your *R* value tell you about the relationship between GNP and life expectancy?

_____

_____

5 Comment on your result.

_____

_____

_____

World outline map

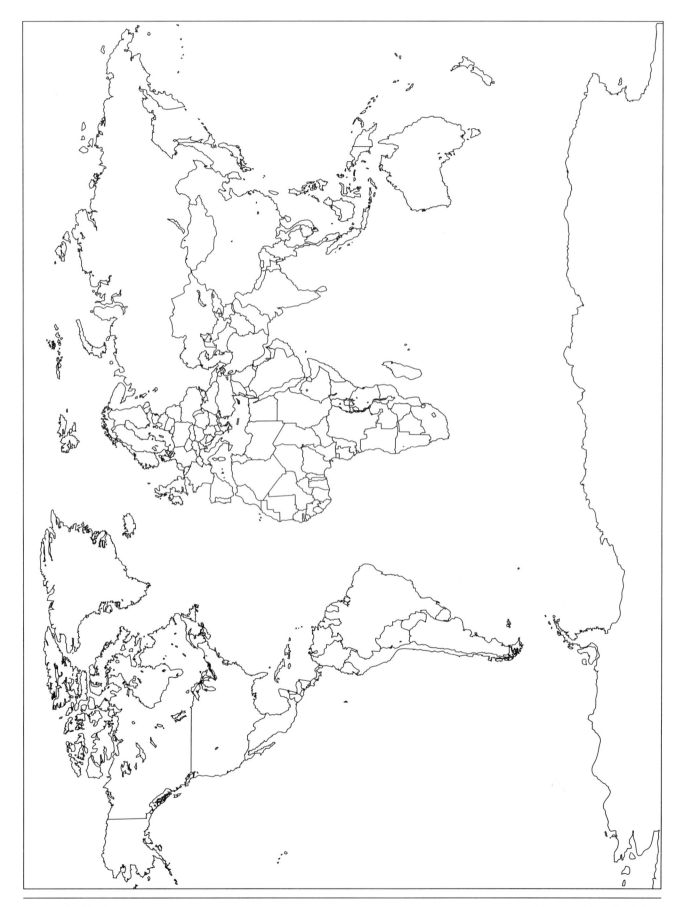

Selected countries: key statistics *(part 1)*

Country	Capital city	Population total 1998	Population density (persons per sq. km) 1998	Birth rate (per 1000 population) 1997	Death rate (per 1000 population) 1997	Life expectancy (years) 1997	Population change (%) 1995–2000	Urban population (%) 1998	Area (sq. km)
Algeria	Algiers	30,081,000	12.6	27	5	70	2.3	59	2,381,741
Australia	Canberra	18,520,000	2.4	14	7	78	1.1	85	7,682,300
Bangladesh	Dhaka	124,774,000	866.5	28	10	58	1.6	23	143,998
Brazil	Brasilia	165,851,000	19.5	21	7	67	1.2	80	8,511,965
Canada	Ottawa	30,563,000	3.1	12	7	79	0.9	77	9,970,610
China	Beijing	1,262,817,000	132.0	17	8	70	0.9	31	9,562,000
Ethiopia	Addis Ababa	59,649,000	52.6	46	20	43	3.2	17	1,133,880
France	Paris	58,683,000	107.9	12	9	78	0.3	75	543,965
Germany	Berlin	82,133,000	229.5	10	10	77	0.3	87	357,868
India	New Delhi	982,223,000	298.8	27	9	63	1.6	28	3,287,263
Indonesia	Jakarta	206,338,000	107.5	24	8	65	1.5	39	1,919,445
Iran	Tehran	65,758,000	39.9	22	6	69	2.2	61	1,648,000
Japan	Tokyo	126,281,000	334.3	10	7	80	0.2	79	377,727
Mexico	Mexico City	95,831,000	48.6	25	5	72	1.6	74	1,972,545
Mozambique	Maputo	18,880,000	23.6	41	20	45	2.5	38	799,380
Nicaragua	Managua	4,807,000	37.0	32	5	68	2.6	55	130,000
Nigeria	Abuja	106,409,000	115.2	40	12	54	2.8	42	923,768
Russian Federation	Moscow	147,434,000	8.6	9	14	67	–0.3	77	17,075,400
Saudi Arabia	Riyadh	20,181,000	9.2	35	4	71	3.4	85	2,200,000
South Africa, Republic of	Pretoria/ Cape Town	39,357,000	32.3	25	8	65	2.2	53	1,219,080
Spain	Madrid	39,628,000	78.5	9	10	78	0.1	77	504,782
Sweden	Stockholm	8,875,000	19.7	10	11	79	0.3	83	449,964
Tanzania	Dodoma	32,102,000	34.0	41	16	48	2.3	31	945,087
United Kingdom	London	58,649,000	240.3	12	11	77	0.1	89	244,082
United States of America	Washington	274,028,000	27.9	15	8	76	0.8	77	9,809,386

Selected countries: key statistics (part 2)

Country	Cultivated area (000s sq. km)	Forest (000s sq. km) 1995	Adult literacy (%) 1998	School enrolment (secondary gross) 1997	Doctors (per 100,000 persons)	Food intake calories (per capita per day) 1997	Energy consumption (million tonnes of oil equivalent) 1997	Trade balance (millions US $) 1999	GNP per capita 1998
Algeria	80	19	61.5	63	83	2,853	26.5	2,200	1,550
Australia	531	409	100.0	153	250	3,224	101.6	-12,850	20,300
Bangladesh	82	10	40.1	19	18	2,086	24.3	-3,410	350
Brazil	653	5,511	84.0	50	134	2,974	172.0	-3,760	4,570
Canada	457	2,446	97.0	108	221	3,119	238.0	18,190	20,020
China	1,354	1,333	83.3	71	115	2,897	1,113.1	29,210	750
Ethiopia	105	-	36.0	12	4	1,858	17.1	-890	100
France	195	150	99.0	111	280	3,518	247.5	9,600	24,940
Germany	121	107	100.0	102	319	3,382	347.3	67,890	25,850
India	1,699	650	53.3	49	48	2,496	461.0	-8,030	430
Indonesia	310	1,098	85.5	52	12	2,886	138.8	24,570	680
Iran	194	15	74.5	74	90	2,836	108.3	2,550	1,770
Japan	43	251	100.0	106	177	2,932	514.9	108,740	32,380
Mexico	273	554	91.0	63	107	3,097	141.5	-11,530	3,970
Mozambique	32	169	42.0	7	<5	1,832	7.7	-1,210	210
Nicaragua	27	56	67.5	47	82	2,186	2.6	-1,330	390
Nigeria	307	138	60.9	34	21	2,735	88.7	930	300
Russian Federation	1,280	7,635	99.0	86	380	2,904	592.0	33,200	2,300
Saudi Arabia	38	2	66.5	61	166	2,783	98.4	20,550	-
South Africa, Republic of	163	85	84.5	84	59	2,990	107.2	-120	2,880
Spain	192	84	97.0	132	400	3,310	107.3	-35,530	14,080
Sweden	28	244	100.0	139	299	3,194	51.9	16,360	25,620
Tanzania	40	325	73.4	5	4	1,995	14.3	-770	210
United Kingdom	64	24	100.0	133	164	3,276	228.0	-52,300	21,400
United States of America	1,790	2,125	99.0	97	245	3,699	2,162.2	-364,850	29,340

Flooding in Mozambique *(part 1)*

In February and March 2000, Mozambique and its neighbouring countries (Figure 1) suffered the worst floods for forty years. Torrential rains associated with tropical storms, including Cyclone Eline (see Figure 2), dumped huge quantities of water on the country, turning river floodplains into vast lakes many tens of kilometres wide and up to 5 m deep.

Over one million people were left homeless by the flooding and hundreds were killed. Rescue work was slow to get under way owing to the lack of helicopters and emergency supplies, much of which had to be brought in from South Africa. As the waters slowly receded, diseases such as dysentery and cholera spread rapidly among those in refugee camps.

1 Look at Atlas Map B (pages 12–13).

a Label the countries on Figure 1. Name the oceans on your map and the line of latitude shown by the broken line.

b Use a blue colour to lightly shade the following countries that were badly affected by the flooding:

- Mozambique
- South Africa
- Zimbabwe
- Zambia
- Madagascar
- Botswana

2 Read the account in Figure 2.

a Describe the effects of Cyclone Eline.

_____

_____

_____

b Why was the storm so intense?

_____

_____

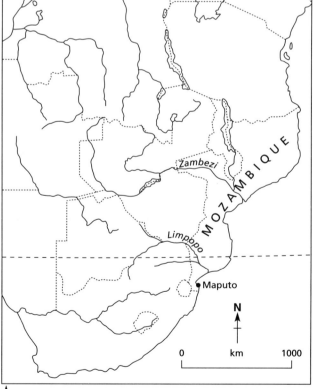

▲ *Figure 1 Mozambique and its neighbours*

Figure 2 Newspaper report about Cyclone Eline ▶

CYCLONE ELINE DRENCHES FLOOD-WEARY MOZAMBIQUE

Cyclone Eline lashed waterlogged Mozambique with gale-force winds and more torrential rain. The storm made landfall from the Indian Ocean and authorities fear that the rains could force the swollen Limpopo River to once again burst its banks and flood vast areas along the border between Zimbabwe and South Africa and through central Mozambique.

Tens of thousands of people were driven from their sodden homes in Mozambique as the country braced for the full force of the tropical cyclone. Corrugated iron roofs were torn from houses as the port town of Beira experienced wind gusts of up to 260 km/h (160 mph).

Most people in the city and in parts of Mozambique evacuated to secure shelters as the cyclone made its way inland. Meteorologists said that high temperatures in the Indian Ocean were increasing the strength of the storm, which left seven dead and thousands homeless as it swept over the island of Madagascar on Friday.

Flooding in Mozambique *(part 2)*

1 Table 1 contains data that compares the rainfall recorded for February 2000 with the average rainfall for a number of towns in southern Mozambique.

Complete the final column of the table to compare the two sets of data. The first one has been done for you.

$1000 / 281 \times 100 = 356\%$

2 Read through the extract about the flooding in Figure 1.

a Apart from loss of life and homelessness, what were the other effects of the flooding on Mozambique?

_____

_____

_____

_____

_____

_____

_____

_____

b Mozambique is one of the poorest countries in the world. How do you think that this contributed to the scale of the problem?

_____

_____

_____

_____

Extension activity

Carry out an Internet search for information about the floods in Mozambique. The aid agencies (e.g. Oxfam, Christian Aid, CAFOD) have reports, as do newspapers. NASA has satellite photos of cyclones that are well worth viewing. A search for Cyclone Eline will reveal hundreds of sites.

Figure 1 ▶
Facts about the flooding of Mozambique

ALL AFRICA NEWS AGENCY
10 March 2000
Maputo – Here are a few facts relating to the flooding situation: 20,000 people in the capital are estimated to have lost their homes due to the flooding.
In the country in general, the number of people directly affected by the floods has risen to 900,000, of whom 300,000 have been displaced from their homes.
At least 200 people have died in the flooding.
The economic losses are enormous. The vital main road N1, which is the only connection between northern and southern parts of the country, is severely damaged, and the general infrastructure is in ruins.
Over 100,000 hectares of crops have been washed away, and over 40,000 head of cattle have drowned.
Mozambique is asking for US$ 10 million to help in reconstructing the country. However, Mozambique is every year spending the same amount to pay for its foreign debt.
Mozambique is a poor but advancing country. Of the total population of 17 million, 45 per cent are aged 14 years or under, 60 per cent of the adult population is illiterate, and life expectancy at birth is only 42.3 years, according to the National Statistics Institute.

▼ *Table 1 Some rainfall statistics*

Town	Total February 2000 rainfall (mm)	Average February rainfall (mm)	February 2000 as percentage of average
Graskop	1000	281	356
Tzaneen (Grenshoek)	1163	177	
Letsitele	498	93	
Phalaborwa	338	83	
Louis Trichardt	669	108	
Levubu	1212	176	
Thohoyandou	1010	108	
Soekmekaar	674	140	

Hurricane tracking chart

Studying the refugee issue using the Internet

The aim of this Internet activity is to find out more about the plight of refugees around the world. To do this you will be using the official United Nations High Commission for Refugees' Website.

Access the Website home page at www.unhcr.ch

1 Find out about some recent examples of refugee movements. To do this click 'Today's News'. Record information about a selection of the refugee movements in Table 1 below.

	Refugee movement (i.e. countries)	Numbers of refugees	Reasons for migration
1			
2			
3			
4			
5			
6			
7			
8			
9			
10			

2 Use Atlas Maps A and B (pages 10–13) to show the migrations on a world outline map (see Sheet 61). Use arrows to show the migrations and either label each one or add a colour key alongside the map.

3 Click on to 'Images' and scan through a selection of the photographs, taking time to read the captions. Make a list of some of the problems faced by refugees.

4 Click on 'Environment'. Make a list of some of the environmental problems associated with refugee movements.

Extension activity
Research your own case study of a refugee movement. Click on to 'The World' and choose a country that interests you. Find out as much as you can about your chosen migration and produce a neat report, including a map. If possible, produce your report using ICT.

Outline map of China

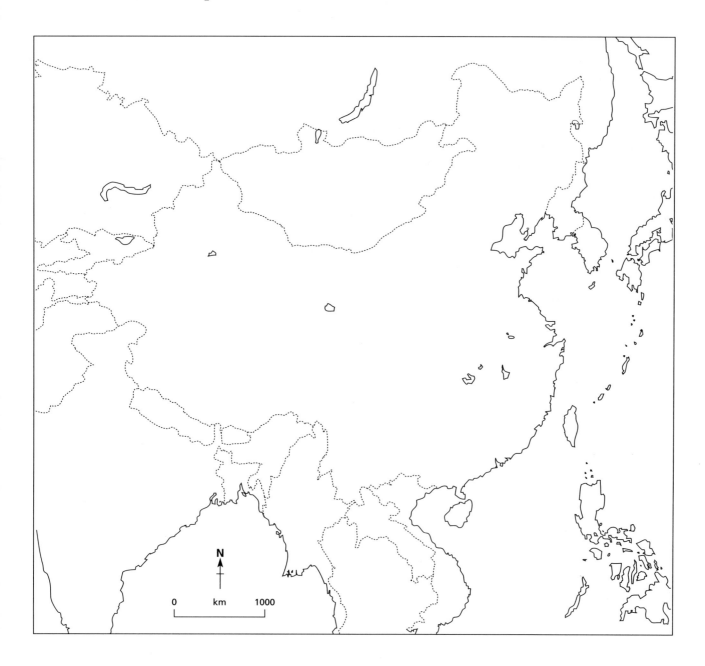

Plotting earthquakes: an ICT activity *(part 1)*

The aim of this activity is to obtain up-to-date information about significant earthquakes from around the world and, by plotting them on a world map, identify which plate margins are particularly active.

1 Contact the National Earthquake Information Center at wwwneic.cr.usgs.gov. If this address fails, conduct a search to find the Center run by the United States Geological Survey (USGS).

2 Click '2001 Large Earthquakes' or the latest year available.

3 Click '2001 Significant Earthquakes of the World' or the latest year available. This will give you a table listing those earthquakes measuring in excess of 6.5 on the Richter Scale or having caused fatalities.

4 Choose the 20 most significant earthquakes and complete Table 1 below.

▼ *Table 1 Significant global earthquakes 2001*

	Date	Location	Magnitude	Region	Comments
1					
2					
3					
4					
5					
6					
7					
8					
9					
10					
11					
12					
13					
14					
15					
16					
17					
19					
20					

Plotting earthquakes: an ICT activity *(part 2)*

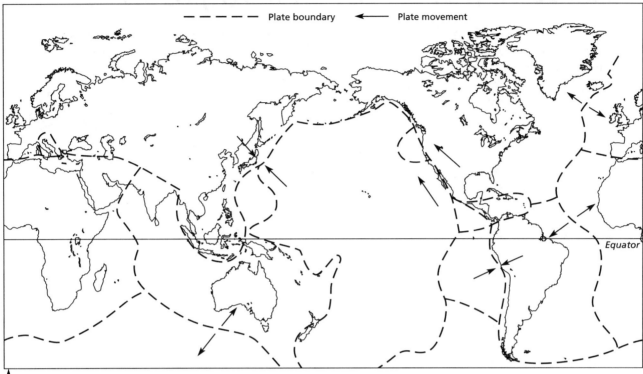

Plate boundary ← Plate movement

Equator

▲ *Figure 1 Earthquake locations*

1 Use Atlas Map B (pages 12–13) to help you plot the locations of your 20 earthquakes on the world map Figure 1.

2 Use Figure 2.2 on page 47 to name the plates.

3 Write a few sentences describing the pattern of your earthquakes. Which plate margins seem to have been most active?

_____

_____

_____

_____

_____

_____

Extension activity

Carry out a similar exercise for volcanoes, either using the data in Table 2.5 on page 49 or using the Volcano World Website (http://volcano.und.nodak.edu) to obtain information about recent eruptions.

Ecotourism in the Manu Biosphere Reserve, Peru: an ICT investigation

The aim of this activity is for you to use the Internet to produce a single-sided brochure/poster encouraging ecotourists (people interested in seeing the natural world managed in a sustainable way) to visit the Manu Biosphere Reserve.

1 Read the information in Figure 1, which will give you some background details about the reserve.

2 Conduct an Internet search by typing Manu Biosphere Reserve. You will come across a number of companies offering small group tours, e.g. http://www.tribes.co.uk/Pe_H_Manu.htm. These will give you an idea of what the attractions are, and you will also come across photographs of the area. In addition, there are several UNESCO-linked sites with information about the reserve, e.g. http://www.wcmc.org.uk/protected_areas/data/wh/manu.html.

3 Produce your brochure, preferably electronically by creating a Word document, to include descriptions of the attractions together with photographs and maps. Take time to design your brochure.

▼ *Figure 2 Location of the Manu Biosphere Reserve, Peru*

Extension work

There are a great many Websites offering details about ecotourism projects, and you may wish to make your own study. Try the following sites to find many useful links:

http://www.ecotourism.about.com/travel/ecotourism
http://www.ecotourism.org.

▼ *Figure 1 The Manu Biosphere Reserve, Peru*

The Manu Biosphere Reserve is situated in southern Peru, in the eastern foothills of the Andes mountains (Figure 2). It was designated a world heritage site in 1987 because of the incredible diversity of the plants and wildlife in the reserve.

The park, which extends down from precipitous mountains at 4000 m in altitude, is situated entirely within the Amazon River basin. Much of the park is relatively low lying and hilly. The area has a wide range of climates, from the cold, dry Andes, to the hot, humid Amazon forests. With a park the size of Manu, which has a wide range of altitude, vegetation varies widely. The most widespread vegetation types found are tropical rainforest in the wetter lowlands, and grassland in the drier highlands.

The reserve protects over 1000 species of birds and some 16,000 plants. About 600 Machiguenga Indians live in the reserve, and they have been involved in some of the tourist developments. For example, the Casa Machiguenga rainforest lodge was built by the Indians, and all profits from the lodge go to the Machiguenga communities located deeper in the park. The Machiguengas are being helped to learn how to run the lodge themselves.

The reserve is managed in a sustainable way. Only a few tourists are allowed access, and then only within a limited area of the reserve. Access to large tracts of the reserve is restricted to scientists only.

Map of the Masai Mara National Reserve

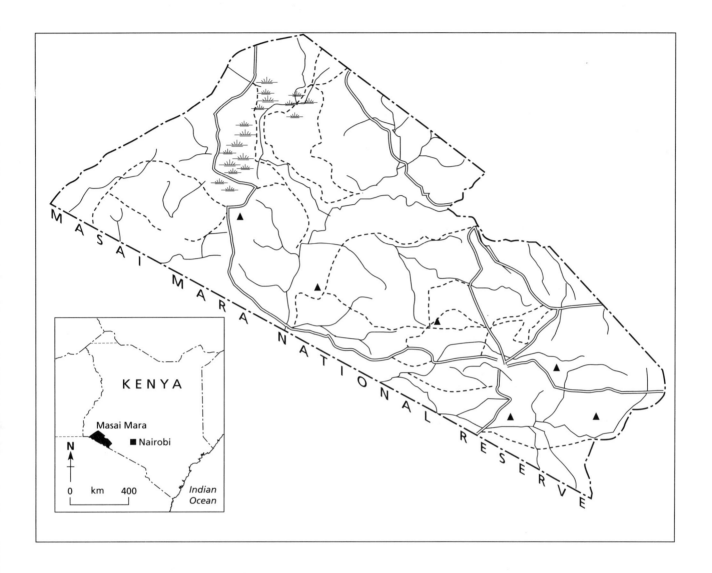

Supporting street children in Brazil

The aim of this activity is to design an advertisement to be published in a teenage British magazine, appealing for money to help street children in Brazil. Ideally, you should work in small groups of twos or threes.

Work through the following stages to produce your advertisement:

A   *Background knowledge.* Read through Figure 1 to discover more about the problem of street children in Brazil. Write down some words that describe what you think life is like for them.

B   *Preparation.* Use the knowledge that you have gained about the plight of street children (pages 72–3) to help you decide what information to put in your advert. Look at charity or appeal adverts in newspapers and magazines for some ideas. Decide what you want to do with the money that is raised – people are more likely to donate if they know that something specific is being planned.

C   *Production.* Produce your advert on a large sheet of paper. Think carefully about its layout and try to write a hard-hitting or eye-catching headline. A clear and interesting design is important if people are going to read your advert. If you wish, you could produce your advertisement by using an ICT package.

▼ *Figure 1 Facts and figures*

Street children in Brazil

- There are estimated to be 12 million children working or living on the streets in Brazil. Many live in extreme hardship, without shelter or adequate food, and violence is commonplace.

- Two million children aged 10–15 have become prostitutes.

- 320,000 children under five years old die every year from preventable diseases – that is three every five minutes!

- Twenty-five per cent of all births are to mothers aged 15–19 years old.

Web search

Look on the internet to find further background information. One particularly good site with links to organisations and articles about street children is:

pangaea.org/street_children/kids.htm

Another site specifically about Brazil is:

www.foundation.novartis.com/brazilian_street_children.htm

Pasoh Forest Reserve, Malaysia *(part 1)*

The Pasoh Forest Reserve (Figure 1) is an example of a sustainably managed forest in Malaysia. It is located about 75 km to the east of Kuala Lumpur and contains a variety of land uses, including commercial forest (where logging is controlled so that it is sustainable), sawmills and plantations (mainly oil palms and rubber).

The reserve also contains 600 ha of virgin rainforest, one of the last areas of primary forest left in Malaysia. The rainforest is extremely rich in biodiversity, containing over 800 species of trees and numerous species of birds, plants and animals.

Surrounding the virgin forest is a 'buffer zone' where logging took place some 40 years ago. Together with the virgin forest, it is the subject of considerable scientific study based at the research centre situated in the heart of the reserve.

1 Use a range of colours to make Figure 1 easier to interpret. Don't forget to colour the key.

▼ **Figure 1 Pasoh Forest Reserve** *(Source: Tropical Forests,* **Field Studies Council, 1997)**

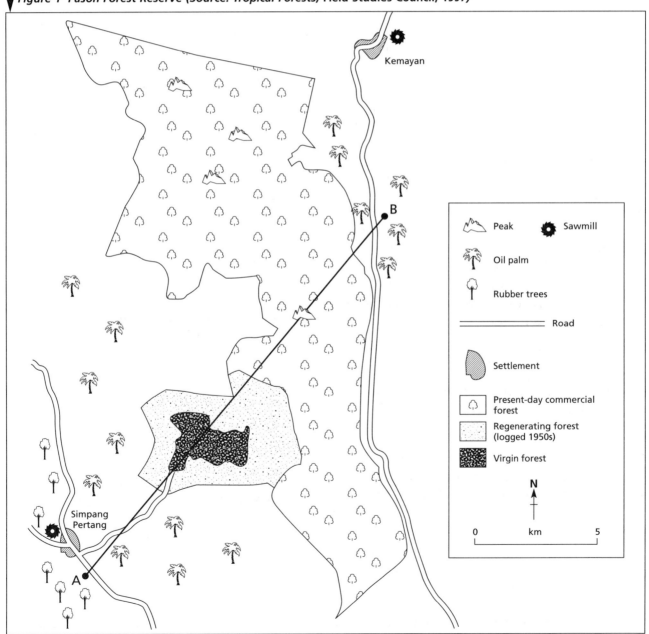

Pasoh Forest Reserve, Malaysia *(part 2)*

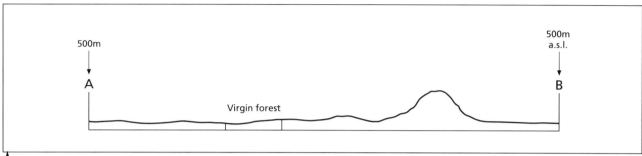

500m

500m
a.s.l.

A

B

Virgin forest

▲ *Figure 1 Cross-section through Pasoh Forest Reserve, A–B* (*Source: Tropical Forests*, Field Studies Council,1997)

1 Figure 1 is a cross-section A–B across the reserve. It shows the relief of the land.

a Lay the straight edge of a piece of paper along the line of section A–B on Figure 1 on Sheet 74.

b Mark the extent of each type of land use on to your piece of paper.

c Now use your paper to plot the different land uses on to the cross-section in Figure 1 above. The virgin forest has been done for you.

d Complete your cross-section by using the same colours used earlier to show the extent of each land use.

2 Attempt the following questions using Figure 1 on Sheet 74 together with your completed cross-section.

a Use the scale on Figure 1 (Sheet 74) to estimate the size (in square kilometres) of the virgin rainforest.

_____

b Roughly how large is the reserve as a whole?

_____

c Why do you think the area that was 'logged in the 1950s' is called a 'buffer zone'?

_____

_____

_____

d Why do you think the buffer zone is the subject of scientific research?

_____

_____

e What is the land outside the Pasoh Forest estate used for?

_____

f Describe the location of the sawmills.

_____

_____

_____

3 What do you understand by the term 'sustainable'?

_____

_____

_____

4 Do you think it is important for forests to be managed sustainably? Why?

_____

_____

_____

Caribbean coral reefs at risk (part 1)

Look at Figure 1. Notice that many of the Caribbean islands, including Jamaica, Bermuda and Puerto Rico, have stretches of coral coastline at serious risk from long-term damage.

Figure 2 describes some of the causes of the damage with specific reference to the Jamaican reefs. Damage to the reefs poses a huge threat to the tourist industry on which most of the islands depend, and some countries, for example Bermuda (Figure 3), are taking steps to improve the situation.

Figure 1 Coral reefs under serious threat in the Caribbean (Source: Reefs at Risk, World Resources Institute) ▼

Figure 3 Bermuda's coral reefs (Source: Reefs at Risk, World Resources Institute) ▼

Signs of progress: Catch levels of grouper and snapper, two important reef species, declined significantly from the mid-1970s, apparently owing to overharvesting. Total grouper catch per fishing pot (a fish trap commonly used to catch reef species) dropped from 1.8 to 0.65 kilos between 1975 and 1985, with smaller fish increasingly predominating. Meanwhile, fish traps and boat anchoring by fishers and recreational boats were damaging reef structure. Under pressure from hotel owners, dive operators, and other businesses, the government closed the $2 million pot fishing industry in 1990, compensating fishers for the cost of their gear and lost revenue. In doing so, Bermuda recognized the importance of its lucrative reef-based tourism and recreational industries – valued at over $9 million in 1988 – while benefitting reef biodiversity in the process.

Source: Reefs at Risk, World Resources Institute

Figure 2 Jamaica's reefs (Source: Reefs at Risk, World Resources Institute) ▼

Description: The entire island is surrounded by reefs, although those of the north coast once contained the most coral cover and are the most diverse. Reefs are an integral part of the Jamaican economy, supporting fishing, and tourism, the country's most important industry.

Threats: Virtually all reef communities here have been affected by human and natural causes. Overfishing in particular, as well as pollution from sewage disposal, industry and agricultural runoff, siltation due to poor land-use practices, and tourism-related activities, have seriously degraded Jamaica's reefs. Storm damage from hurricanes, coral reef bleaching because of periodic high sea water temperatures, and, with the decline of sea urchins and other algae grazers, the unchecked algal overgrowth of corals, have compounded the problem. The reefs surrounding Montego Bay are perhaps the most seriously degraded, even though they are protected, in part, by a marine park. The original park, established in 1966, was too small and was completely unmanaged. Although re-established and expanded in 1990, with a financial base and staff that works closely with town authorities, reefs in the park continue to be affected by poaching, pollution from the nearby city and airport, and runoff from inland agricultural activity.

Source: Reefs at Risk, World Resources Institute

Caribbean coral reefs at risk *(part 2)*

1 Use a red colour or highlight pen to highlight the coral coastlines at greatest risk from damage.

2 Which countries in the Caribbean are under greatest threat of damage to their coral reefs?

_____

_____

3 Read through Figure 2 on Sheet 76.

a Why are the coral reefs that surround Jamaica important to the country's economy?

_____

_____

_____

b List three natural causes and three human causes of damage to the reefs.

Natural 1 _____

 2 _____

 3 _____

Human 1 _____

 2 _____

 3 _____

c Why does the marine park at Montego Bay continue to suffer damage despite being carefully managed?

_____

_____

_____

_____

4 Read Figure 3 on Sheet 76.

a Why were the reefs around Bermuda being damaged?

_____

_____

_____

b Why did the government decide to try to protect the reefs?

_____

_____

_____

_____

c What has the government done?

_____

_____

_____

_____

5 How do you think the Jamaican government could improve the health of its coral reefs?

_____

_____

_____

_____

_____

_____

_____

The cyclone hazard in Bangladesh *(part 1)*

Bangladesh suffers from the effects of tropical cyclones (hurricanes). The heavy rain and strong winds associated with these intense storms (see page 24) have caused massive devastation in low-lying coastal parts of the country, most recently in 1991.

1 Read through the newspaper article in Figure 1 and answer the following questions.

a How many people living on the coast are thought to be at risk from a future cyclone?

_____

b How many cyclone shelters existed before 1991?

_____

c How many people lost their lives in the 1991 cyclone?

_____

d How many people are unable to take shelter in a cyclone shelter?

_____

e Apart from sheltering in a cyclone shelter, what else do people do to seek shelter?

_____

2 Why is it important to improve education about cyclone preparedness and to make sure that there are good communication systems, particularly in rural areas?

_____

_____

_____

_____

_____

Figure 1 Newspaper report (Source: Independent of Bangladesh, 3 February 2000) ▼

MILLIONS AT RISK FROM FUTURE CYCLONE

Around 70 lakh (pronounced 'lark') people living in the country's coastline are not fully protected against deadly cyclones and tidal surges that batter the areas often. If any cyclone with the intensity of the one that ravaged coastal areas on 29 April 1991 hits the region, loss of life and property along the 710-kilometre coastline might be severe.

At present there are 1841 cyclone shelters; 1300 of them were built after the 1991 titanic cyclone which left at least one lakh 33 thousand people dead. Thirteen lakh people, out of one crore ten lakh who live in the disaster-prone areas, can take shelter in the cyclone shelters during the time of any impending disaster. Thirty-three lakh people are able to move to safer places of their own during an emergency, but about 70 lakh people remain helpless as they have no high-rise building or ground in their vicinity where they can move to.

According to the Meteorological Department, at least 34 cyclones had ravaged the country's coastline over the last four decades since 1960, claiming about five lakh 50 thousand lives. Despite a programme of shelter building and disaster preparation, some people are unhappy about what has been done. Kabir Ahmed, who lives in a small village on the Bay of Bengal, has complained that 'the damaged embankments have not yet been repaired, people are not aware of the actions of cyclone preparedness programmes, and improvement in the communication network [to give warnings] is yet to see light'. A lack of money within Bangladesh is being blamed for the slow programme of cyclone shelter building.

(Note: 'lakh' = a hundred thousand; and 'crore' = ten million)

The cyclone hazard in Bangladesh *(part 2)*

1 Table 1 describes the annual frequency of cyclone warnings in Bangladesh. Make up your own colour key to show the data in Table 1 by colouring in the appropriate segments in the calendar chart in Figure 1. Look at Skills Box 2 (pages 18–19) to remind you about the choropleth technique.

Write a couple of sentences describing the yearly pattern.

_____

_____

_____

_____

_____

_____

_____

_____

_____

_____

_____

_____

Table 1 *Annual frequency of tropical cyclone warnings in Bangladesh (Source: Cyclone '91, Bangladesh Centre for Advanced Studies)* ▼

Month	J	F	M	A	M	J	J	A	S	O	N	D
Tropical cyclone warnings	1	1	1	9	32	6	8	4	14	32	48	21

▼ **Figure 1** *Calendar chart to show cyclone warnings*

Key

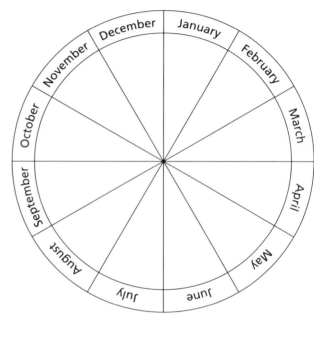

▼ **Figure 2** *A cyclone shelter (Source: The Hawlader Family, ActionAid)*

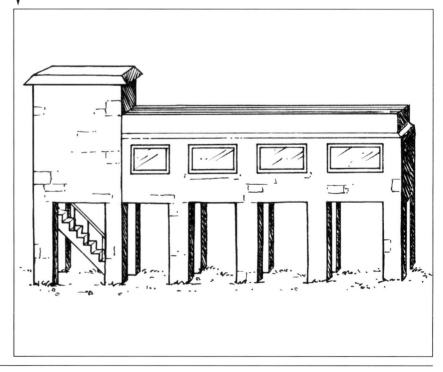

2 Use the information on pages 102–3 to help you to add labels to the sketch of a cyclone shelter in Figure 2.

Aid for Bangladesh

Bangladesh does not have the ability to feed its people and to provide them with basic services such as safe water, sanitation and electricity. Several countries, including the UK, the USA, Canada and Australia, give aid to Bangladesh. Charities such as ActionAid (page 106) and Oxfam (Figure 1) invest money and expertise to help improve conditions.

Farm yields have been increased by the introduction of high-yielding varieties (HYV) of seed. Greater use of fertiliser and irrigation has also enabled crop production to increase, particularly of rice. However, it is only relatively rich farmers who can afford these seeds, and the fertilisers and irrigation methods to make them grow successfully.

The most hopeful sign for the future is the determination of the Bangladeshi people to work hard and to improve their lives, despite the many difficulties that have to be overcome.

1 Study Figure 1. For each of Oxfam's aid measures, suggest reasons why the measure should help to improve living conditions and people's quality of life in Bangladesh.

Flood shelters

_____

_____

_____

Education

_____

_____

_____

Island Development Society

_____

_____

_____

Saptagrams

_____

_____

_____

2 For this activity you can work on your own or in pairs. Your job is to put together an aid programme for Bhola Island. Work through the following steps and then present your aid programme in the form of a neat account or poster.

a Re-read the unit on Bhola Island (pages 104–7) and make a list of some of the problems and issues that need to be addressed.

b Decide on your priorities. What improvements will have the greatest effects on people's lives and on their futures? Try to arrange your list in rank order.

c Now put together your aid package. Try to suggest convincing arguments for them. You do not have access to limitless funds, so be sensible.

▼ *Figure 1 Oxfam in Bangladesh*

- In Sirajgonj district, one of the poorest parts of Bangladesh, Oxfam is working with local people to help them to cope with river floods. Flood shelters have been built, trees planted and community groups set up to help during emergencies.
- Education programmes for children and adults have been introduced. Women are shown how to earn an income – for example, by rearing animals.
- On the island of Hatia (see Atlas Map D, page 95), Oxfam has helped to set up the Island Development Society. The society has established schools and health clinics, and people are given advice to help them to claim ownership of land. Savings groups have been set up and people can borrow money to invest in their land.
- Rural women's groups, locally known as Saptagrams, have been created to help women take charge of their lives and learn new skills. The aim of these groups is to improve the lives of women in a male-dominated society.

Map of Bangladesh

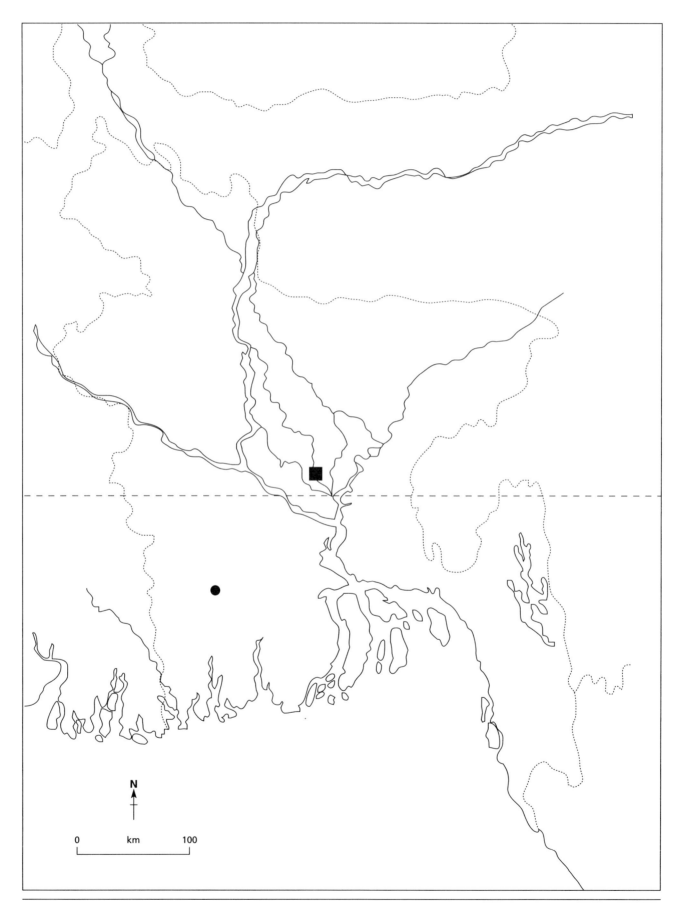

Cotton, from field to fabric

In early spring the cotton fields are ploughed and rolled. Mechanical planters sow the cotton seeds 10 or 12 rows at a time. The planter opens a small trench, drops the right amount of seed and then covers the seed and packs it down. Planting takes place from February onwards.

Machines called 'cultivators' are used to uproot the weeds that compete with the cotton for sunlight and for soil nutrients and water. After about three months the cotton bolls are formed and the white cotton fibres burst forth to dry in the sun.

The cotton is harvested by machines in the autumn and the stalks of the plants are cut down and ploughed into the soil. The cotton is transported for processing to a gin (a separating machine).

At the gin, the cotton is cleaned and the fibres are separated from the seeds. The ginned fibres are pressed together into blocks called 'bales' that weigh about 230 kg. The bales then go to a textile mill to be spun and woven into fabric. Finally, the fabric is sent to a finishing plant to be bleached, dyed and printed before being made into clothing or products for the home. Meanwhile, the seeds are sent from the gin to an oil mill to extract the oil.

1 Use the text alongside to complete a flow diagram (using the boxes in Figure 1) to describe the sequence of events that takes cotton 'from field to fabric'. Add some illustrations of your own and some colour to make the diagram more attractive.

Figure 1 Flow diagram describing cotton, from field to fabric ▼

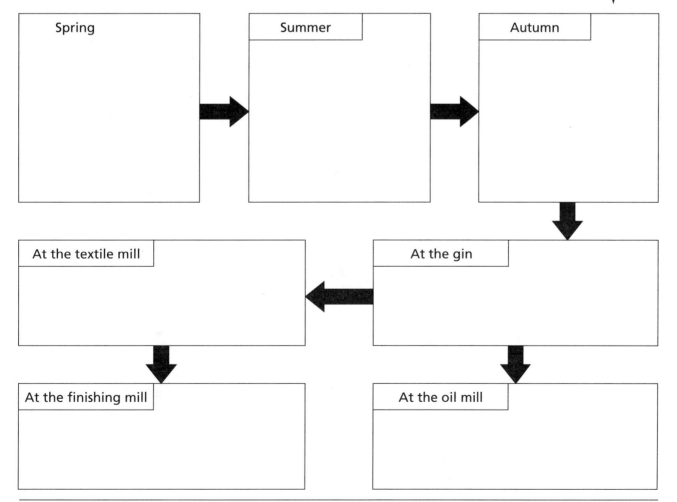

Fisherman's Wharf, San Francisco

Fisherman's Wharf is one of the most popular tourist areas in San Francisco. It is situated in the north-eastern corner of Figure 2.5 (page 119). The attractions of the area are shown in Figure 1.

Either

Design a day's outing in the Fisherman's Wharf area for a family of two adults and two teenage children, one boy and one girl. The boy is keen to visit ships and wants to go swimming. The girl wants to visit the Guinness Book of World Records and go shopping in Ghirardelli Square. The parents are keen to visit Alcatraz and have a Chinese meal in the early evening (the children would rather have a McDonald's!). The family have agreed to spend the whole day together. They are staying at the Hyatt Hotel.

Study Figure 1 and put together a plan, called an 'itinerary', for their day. Decide what they should do in the morning and in the afternoon. You must satisfy their requests but you can add other attractions if you wish. Be careful not to pack too much into their day as they will want to spend some time at each attraction.

Use a coloured line to show your route on Figure 1.

Or

Produce a similar itinerary for yourself or for your family. Give reasons for your choices of attractions.

▼ **Figure 1 Fisherman's Wharf**

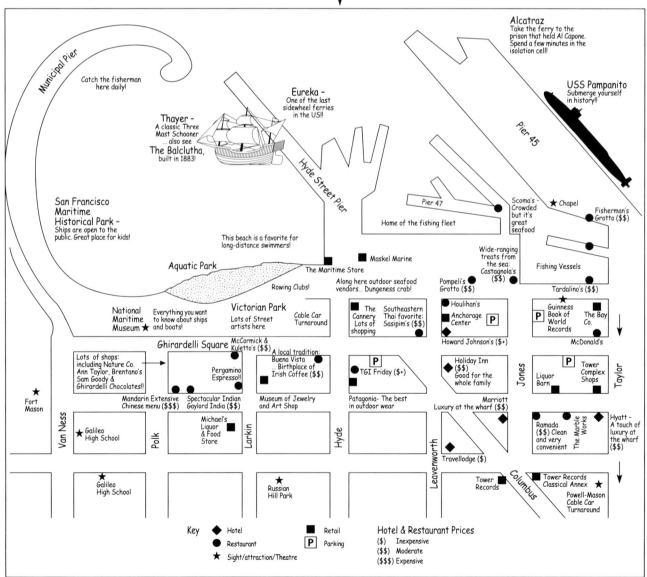

Tornadoes in the United States (part 1)

A tornado is a violent windstorm with a characteristic twisting, funnel-shaped cloud (Figure 1). With wind speeds of up to 500 km/hour, it is one of the most violent and deadly natural hazards on Earth.

A tornado is usually only a few hundred metres across and, as a result, its path of destruction is very narrow. However, it is capable of lifting cars, turning over mobile homes and removing roofs from houses.

Tornadoes occur throughout the world, although the most intense and devastating ones are found in the United States. On average, some 1000 tornadoes are reported every year in the United States. In 1999 there were 1343 tornadoes, making it one of the most violent of recent years. Ninety-four people lost their lives and many millions of dollars' worth of damage was caused.

Tornadoes can occur just about anywhere in the United States, although the majority tend to occur in a central corridor running from Texas, in the south, through Oklahoma and into Kansas. This is known as 'tornado alley'. Figure 1 on Sheet 85 shows the location of the 'killer' tornadoes in 1999 (i.e. those responsible for causing deaths).

Tornadoes are associated with severe and intense thunderstorms. An immense storm cloud may develop a 'funnel cloud' at its base which 'touches down' to form a tornado (Figure 1). A tornado may carve a path of destruction for up to 20 minutes.

Thunderstorms are usually formed when the ground surface becomes hot and the air above it is forced to rise. This process is called 'convection'. The hottest parts of the United States are in the central and southern states because these areas are far away from the cooling influence of the sea. It is these areas that usually experience the greatest number of tornadoes.

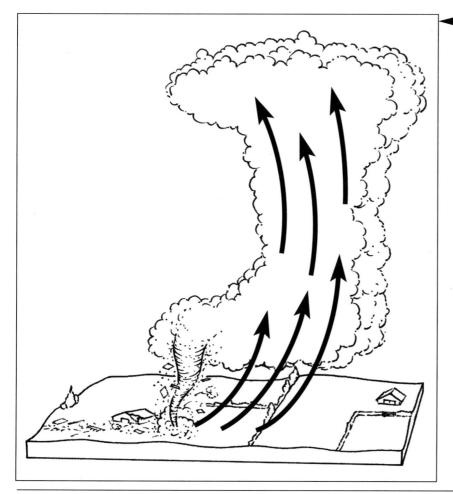

◄ *Figure 1 The formation of a tornado*

1 Study Figure 1. Add the following labels in their correct places:

- tall thunderstorm cloud up to 10,000 metres high;

- funnel-shaped tornado;

- dust and broken fragments whisked around at the base of the tornado;

- rapidly rising air currents due to convection;

- the very narrow path of a tornado on the ground.

Tornadoes in the United States *(part 2)*

▼ *Figure 1 'Killer' tornadoes in the USA, 1999*

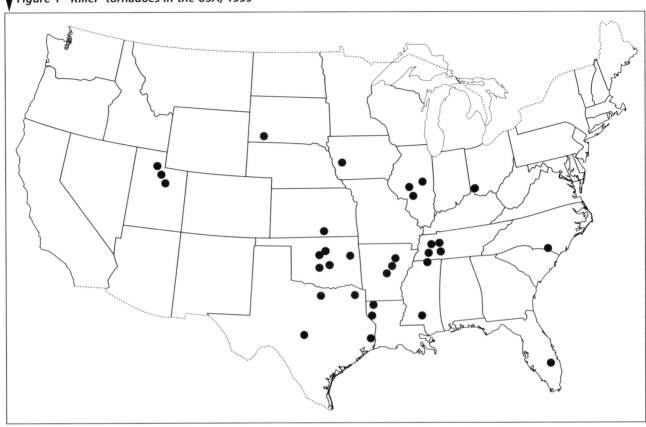

1 Study the map of deadly tornadoes, Figure 1.

a Use Figure 1 and Atlas map E (page 109) to help you describe the distribution of 'killer' tornadoes in 1999. Are they spread evenly across the United States or are they concentrated in certain areas?

_____

_____

_____

_____

b What is 'tornado alley'? Do you think it is an appropriate term?

_____

_____

_____

c Why do so many tornadoes occur in the central and southern states?

_____

_____

_____

_____

_____

_____

d Can you suggest why most tornadoes occur in the early afternoon?

_____

_____

_____

_____

_____

Tornadoes in the United States *(part 3)*

2 Table 1 contains data listing the numbers of tornadoes reported in each month during 1999.

a Draw a bar graph to show this information, using the axes in Figure 2. Give your graph a title.

b Describe the trend of tornadoes during the months of the year. Is there an even spread, or does there seem to be a seasonal pattern?

_____

_____

_____

_____

c In which month was there an unusually high number of tornadoes for the time of year?

_____

d Try to suggest reasons why most tornadoes occur in the summer.

_____

_____

_____

_____

Web search

There are many tornado sites on the Internet:
Storm Prediction Center at
  www.spc.noaa.gov
National Climatic Data Center at
  www.ncdc.noaa.gov
Federal Emergency Management Agency at
  www.fema.gov
Texas Severe Storms Association at
  www.tessa.org
Stormchasers at
  www.tornadochaser.com

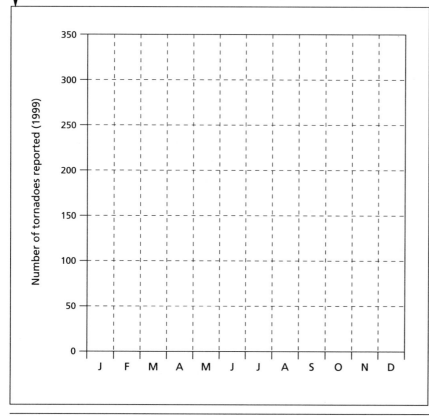

▼*Figure 2 Total reported tornadoes in the USA by month (1999)*

Table 1 Total reported tornadoes in the United States by month (1999) ▼

January	212
February	22
March	56
April	176
May	311
June	289
July	100
August	79
September	56
October	18
November	9
December	15

(*Source:* Storm Prediction Center, NOAA)

The Spencer tornado, 30 May 1998 (part 1)

At 8.40 p.m. on 30 May 1998, the small town of Spencer in South Dakota (see Figure 1) was hit by a powerful tornado. One resident, Mabel Allen, aged 81, survived the tornado in a cupboard under the stairs with six other women. They were among the lucky ones. Six people were killed by the tornado and one-third of the town's 320 residents were injured. Most of the town's 190 buildings were completely destroyed, and an estimated $18 million worth of damage was caused.

That evening a huge thunderstorm had spawned five separate tornadoes during a one- hour period. The one that hit Spencer, whose damage was limited to a track less than 2 km in length, ran straight through the middle of the town.

Warnings of a likely tornado had been broadcast, but the local fire station siren could not be sounded because of a loss of electricity due to the thunderstorm. The last tornado to cause loss of life in South Dakota occured way back in 1970.

Tornadoes cannot be prevented from occurring. Instead, people have to learn to live with the threat that they pose. The National Weather Service produces a list of guidelines to help people survive tornadoes (see Figure 1 on Sheet 88), and warnings of possible tornadoes are given by the media.

1 Look back at the information about the Spencer tornado.

a Why do you think the tornado occured in the early evening and in the summer?

_____

_____

b What do you think Mabel Allen and her friends must have been feeling when the tornado hit the house?

_____

_____

_____

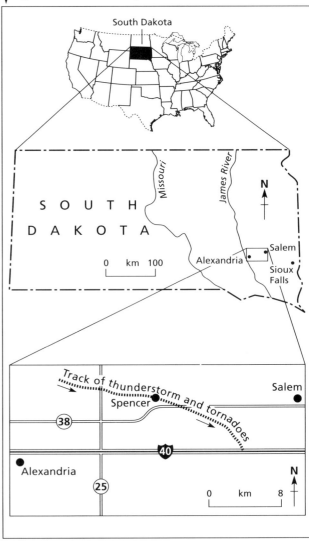

▼ *Figure 1 Location of Spencer, South Dakota*

(*Source : Argus Leader,* www.argusleader.com)

c Given that the siren failed to work, what would you suggest should be done in the future to warn people?

_____

_____

_____

_____

_____

The Spencer tornado, 30 May 1998 *(part 2)*

1 Study Figure 1. Produce a poster, using simple sketches and writing, to describe how people can protect themselves from tornadoes. Take time to plan your poster carefully so that it is attractive to look at, clear and accurate.

▼ *Figure 1 Tornado safety rules (Source:* **NOAA***)*

Tornado safety rules

In Homes, the basement offers the greatest safety. Seek shelter under sturdy furniture if possible. In homes without basements, take cover in the center part of the house, on the lowest floor, in a small room such as a closet or bathroom, or under sturdy furniture. Keep away from windows.

In Shopping Centers, go to a designated shelter area (**not** to your parked car).

In Office Buildings, go to an interior hallway on the lowest floor, or to the designated shelter area.

In Schools, follow advance plans to a designated shelter area, usually an interior hallway on the lowest floor. If the building is not of reinforced construction, go to a nearby one that is, or take cover outside on low, protected ground. Stay out of auditoriums, gymnasiums, and other structures with wide, free-span roofs.

In Automobiles, leave your car and seek shelter in a substantial nearby building, or lie flat in a nearby ditch or ravine.

In Open country, lie flat in the nearest ditch or ravine.

Mobile Homes are particularly vulnerable and should be evacuated. Trailer parks should have a community storm shelter and a warden to monitor broadcasts throughout the severe storm emergency. If there is no shelter nearby, leave the trailer and take cover on low, protected ground.

The USA and its states

Outline map of the USA

N

0   km   1000

The basic geography of the USA

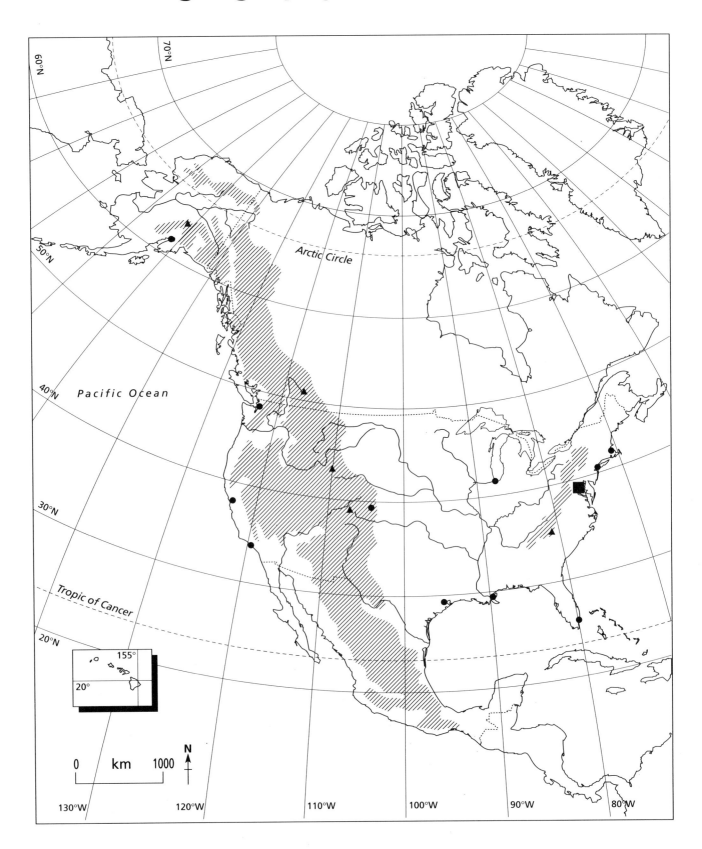